YOLANDA DREWELL

LOOK, FEEL & AGE FABULOUS

For Intrepid Women:
An Invigorating Perspective
On Self-Confidence, *Fabulosity*
And Other Midlife Antics

FABULOUS
PUBLISHING
CO

PRAISE FOR THE BOOK

I absolutely loved reading Look, Feel & Age Fabulous!!! I'm not sure where to start with so many positive comments. I loved that the author made the book personal with her own experience growing up and where she is in her life today. She introduced her family and the journey she is on.

It is most definitely the way I have decided (mostly in the last few years) to always be looking for joy and happiness and saying yes to anything that comes along. Always learning, always finding new things to discover even at 72 because age is just a number!

I felt that so many of her phrases were Fabulous, and I found myself rereading to make sure her words were registering. I had already applied some of the language and made small changes in my life, like no negativity in how I react to things, and I carefully choose the people I want to be around. In the book I had an 'ahh-ha' moment when reading about the author's podcast with Johanna White. It was an honor to read this book and I'm so glad I found the *Fabulosity* movement.

PAULINE BARNS

I loved reading this book, and it felt as if the author were talking to me personally. A few things were eye-openers for me, like when she talks about feeling the odd one out and realizing everyone in that group felt the odd one out. There were so many things I recognized in myself, but I also realized that over the years I have become, and am becoming, more of the person I want to be. Maybe this has to do with age and caring less about what other people think. I felt the book was inviting me in and making me curious.

It invites women to think about how they want to, (or can) live their lives.

I love the optimistic language she uses and words I have never come across before, like *Fabulosity*, figureoutable or fabuli.

This book oozes personality. I like that a lot.

Highly recommended.

MONIQUE GOULD

I just finished reading this book, and I really enjoyed it !

I absolutely love the definition of *Fabulosity* and how the author works through each element of it. And the acronyms YTB and FIFI! There are so many golden nuggets in this book, and a lot of what she says resonates with my approach to life and how I coach my clients.

The self-identity part is key. I think every woman needs more *Fabulosity* in her life!

CELIA CONRAD

A book for those who are looking for a simple philosophy to live their lives by. Fabulosity has very few rules, is expansive in its thinking, and is accessible with the how-to's which, when implemented, will have far-reaching impacts. Never more to disappear from life after 50 into invisible, old age!

VANESSA VAN WYK

A fun and uplifting overview of how to live a bigger, more vivacious midlife. Peppered with personal experiences and wisdom throughout, this uplifting book promotes positivity, self-expression, and living your best life ...all whilst being proudly, imperfectly, and courageously YOU.

It's the perfect antidote to toxic societal messages that leave too many amazing midlife women feeling beige, past it, or washed out.

Never fear, Yolanda is here to help you *Fabify* your life!

SAMANTHA JENKINS

Wow! What a ride! I really enjoyed this book! I loved the whole concept of the *Fabosphere* and embracing midlife with joy and happiness. It's such a difficult time for so many of us and you just made me want to embrace my own *Fabulosity* and embrace life to the absolute fullest. If midlife and the menopause has sucked the life out of you and you need something to kick you up proverbial, shake you up and take you to the '*Fabosphere*' (aka a world of fabulousness) then this is the read for you.

JULIA WITHERSPOON

Could I live a life of 'Fabulosity'? I had never even thought about it, however, having read Yolanda Drewell's book, the question I now ask myself is, "Why on earth would I not want to?" I was hooked! I want to, and am going to, live my life to the fullest- by looking, feeling, and doing Fabulous. In the most creative, honest, engaging, and energizing way, you will be guided and supported as you achieve the new you. This easy-to-read, frank, and fun book is one you will read, go back to, share with others, and never part with.

TERRY DEARLING

An inspiring story, that goes beyond a motivational book. It's like a close dialogue with a good friend, her doubts, fears and most authentic emotions, which deep down are those of anyone who seeks to deepen their own self. But for that you have to be brave. That is what it is about, to get to know the most authentic part of ourselves, with enthusiasm, courage and why not having fun breaking the rules.

MARGA SANZ

© Copyright Yolanda Drewell 2023 - All rights reserved.

The content within this book may not be reproduced, duplicated or transmitted without direct written permission from the author or the publisher.

Under no circumstances will any blame or legal responsibility be held against the publisher, or author, for any damages, reparation, or monetary loss due to the information contained within this book. Either directly or indirectly. You are responsible for your own choices, actions, and results.

Legal Notice:

This book is copyright protected. This book is only for personal use. You cannot amend, distribute, sell, use, quote or paraphrase any part, of the content within this book, without the consent of the author or publisher.

Disclaimer Notice:

Please note the information contained within this document is for educational and entertainment purposes only. All effort has been expended to present accurate, up-to-date, and reliable, complete information. No warranties of any kind are declared or implied. Readers acknowledge that the author is not engaging in the rendering of legal, financial, medical or professional advice. The content within this book has been derived from various sources. Please consult a licensed professional before attempting any techniques outlined in this book.

By reading this document, the reader agrees that under no circumstances is the author responsible for any losses, direct or indirect, which are incurred as a result of the use of the information contained within this document, including, but not limited to, — errors, omissions, or inaccuracies.

This book is dedicated to:

All the world's Fabulous women
who want to live their next chapter
on their own terms.

My amazing husband and children
who inspire, challenge and
cheerlead me every day.

The incredible network of amazing women
and men who continue to have faith in me,
even on the days when I have little faith
of my own.

CONTENTS

♥ Special Invitation — XI

PART I — XII

Welcome To Fabulous — 1
Four Decisions — 5
Wanted: Role Models — 19

PART II — 22

Hello Queen Of Fabulosity — 23
You 2.0 — 31

PART III — 36

Introducing... Fabulosity — 37
What Fabulosity Isn't — 75
The Three Permissions — 81

PART IV — 100

The Fabuli Archetype — 101
The FIFI Formula — 111
Conclusion — 133

PART V — 136

The Rabbi's Gift — 137
♥ Help Others Find Their Fabulous — 140

A Tribute To Every Woman

In a world where dreams unfurl,
Where strength and grace intertwine,
Let us celebrate every woman's worth,
Her essence, divine.

From dawn's first light to twilight's glow,
Her spirit soars, her passions grow.
In fields of science, art, and lore,
She weaves her magic, forevermore.

She walks the path of countless queens,
Embracing roles, breaking through screens,
A mother's love, a sister's care,
Her gentle touch, beyond compare.

In boardrooms filled with fierce debate,
She stands unyielding, strong and great.
A leader bold, her voice rings clear,
Inspiring others, dispelling fear.

She fights for justice, bound by truth,
Her voice a beacon, resolute.
From humble homes to war-torn lands,
Her courage burns, forever stands.

In classrooms where young minds ignite,
She fuels their dreams, a guiding light.
A teacher, mentor, imparting knowledge,
Igniting flames of wisdom in each college.

In every dance, in every song,
Her spirit dances, free and strong
An artist's brush, a poet's pen,
Her creations stir the souls of men.

She bears the weight of countless roles,
A nurturer of hearts and souls.
In her embrace, we find our rest,
A sanctuary, a love expressed.

In every corner of the earth,
Her presence blooms, her beauty birthed.
From east to west, and near and far,
She shines as bright as every star.

So let us raise our voices high,
In homage to the women who defy,
The limits placed upon their worth,
Each one a miracle at birth.

For in their dreams, the world awakes,
As every woman's spirit takes,
Its rightful place, forever true,
Acknowledged, honored, all for you.

Anon

SPECIAL INVITE

 Special Invitation

Hey Gorgeous Lady!

I'm so excited to welcome you to the *Fabosphere*.

This is where amazing, gorgeous, positive women just like you and me hang out.

Before you dive into this book, I'd like to invite you to start your *fabulous* journey with a special welcome video message from me.

You can find it on a secret page on my website, along with some other free bonuses related to the book.

Here is the special link and QR code:

yolandadrewell.com/lfaf

There you will also be invited to stay connected with me and my team so that you don't miss out on any future fabulousness as it unfolds.

I hope you enjoy the book!
x Yolanda

PART I

#FBLS IS THE WAY

Welcome To Fabulous

This book is based on my titillating and compelling proposition that one word—"fabulous"—can change your life in the most delicious way.

By using it on a daily basis—both verbally and energetically—"fabulous" can open the door to elevating and activating your energy, confidence, and resilience. I know that it can, because I'm proof of it.

For me, the love of this word has evolved into a life philosophy called, you guessed it, fabulosity, which is a word that already exists, but I've given it a new lease on life.

I've revitalized and upgraded it, and, from now on, it and all its direct relations shall be capitalized and italicized!

Fabulosity has become a habit. I live by it on a daily basis as a way of challenging myself to keep exploring and expanding beyond my comfort zone and into the *Fabosphere*.

> *Finding Fabulosity has been so life-changing that I want to share it with other women who might also find it a delicious way to go through life, hence this book.*

I'm not an experienced author, but I chose not to have this book professionally ghostwritten because I wanted my voice to come through loud and strong, imperfectly but authentically, in the spirit of *Fabulosity*.

So, I took on the "identity" of an author and launched myself into writing this book, ready or not, because I felt compelled and excited to do it. I haven't held back, and I hope that it will delight and inspire you to find the freedom to also launch into new frontiers, simply because you feel compelled and excited to - without overthinking, overlearning, or waiting.

By approaching any of life's projects in this intuitive, happy-go-lucky way, we are embodying the core values of *Fabulosity*, which are courage, authenticity, activation, freedom, spontaneity, and pleasure.

These values are ever-evolving because, like us, *Fabulosity* cannot be put into a box, and this is one of its delights. But I'm getting ahead of myself!

In this book, I'll explain what *Fabulosity* is, what it's not, who can access it, and how.

I'll share how it became a habit and life philosophy for me and what it looks like day-to-day.

> *Everything you read is my perspective on living in a way where women can look, feel, and age "Fabulous" without youth, wealth, Botox, fashion rules, or dieting. Oh, the freedom of that!*

Be warned, I use the word "*Fabulous*" an awful lot in this book because, a lot of the time, there just isn't another word that encapsulates all of its juiciness.

This book is not "the answer," and I'm not in any shape or form a know-it-all guru who wants to "show the way to *Fabulosity*" to everyone else.

> *I think of myself as a cheerleader, and my hope is that I can inspire, challenge, and cheerlead you to be bigger and bolder in your life, and I want you to live with more freedom, fun, and spontaneity in splendid fashion. If, like me, that's what you're after!*

If this book triggers you in any way or you find yourself believing that the state of *Fabulosity* is out of reach for whatever reason, please seek help.

Do what you must to shift into a frame of mind that makes it possible to rediscover your verve and where you can get moving into the state of feeling GREAT!

Except for a few fundamentals, the most delicious thing about this intriguing life philosophy is that it's totally relative. Your version of looking, feeling, and living *Fabulous* could be entirely different from mine.

At the time of writing, I personally have found that *Fabulosity* for me is about dressing more flamboyantly, taking to the stage, and meeting as many inspiring women as possible offline, as well as online through my podcast, Fabulous To Meet You.

This all might sound horrendous to you. Your version of *Fabulosity* might be to take up art lessons for the first time in your life or start a school. Perhaps you want to solo travel, or swim in the sea without feeling self-conscious about your body. These are all awesome and *Fabulous* if they feel important to you.

> *This book is for women from all walks of life who are looking to break free from expectations—everyone else's as well as their own—and to simply LOVE the experience of the life they're living, warts and all.*

Like this book, perfection doesn't exist, so finding the *Fabulous* in the life we have while we create the life we want is exactly the point. *Fabulosity* is both a journey and a destination, and I remind myself of this every day.

The *Fabulous* perspective is not for everyone, and if it's not for you, no worries. Simply close the book and perhaps pass it on to someone else who might get a kick out of it. I get that it's a somewhat jaunty way of being and thinking, and I've met with a few blank stares over the last year when I've tried to explain my *Fabulous* mission!

However, so many more women like the boldness and free-spiritedness of the *Fabulous* message and feel enlivened by the idea of living in the *Fabosphere*!

The *Fabosphere* is a wonderful place.

It's like that feeling in your stomach when you're in love or you're so excited about something.

Or when you have intense feelings of pride for your child, or absolute love for your dog or cat.

It's like being swept up by the most incredible cloud of bliss, made of self-love, delight at being alive in this moment, and blissful anticipation for what's coming next—even if you don't know what that is.

The *Fabosphere* is THOSE feelings and more.

It's a scintillating place to hang out.

It's full of positivity, freedom, glee, camaraderie, expansiveness, and curiosity.

Are you intrigued?

I hope so. Without further ado, let's get started!

Four Decisions

If we haven't met before, I'm Yolanda Drewell, the Chief Instigator of the *Fabulosity* Movement, and I'm also known as the Queen of *Fabulosity*.

I'm a South African mother of four; the wife of Mark, a British entrepreneur; and I'm the owner of two delightful poodles and an ancient but sprightly cat. I was born in Johannesburg to Dutch parents, with my Dutch roots contributing to my candid, straight-talking manner.

Despite this, as a child and teenager, I was quite introverted and spent a lot of time on my own, drawing or reading. I had a handful of close friends, but I wasn't part of the popular set, and I never really wanted to be. I've always had an unconventional perspective on the world with a knack for seeing through complexity (and B.S.), and throughout my life, I've often felt like the odd one out. I'm smiling to myself as I write because I've just remembered a little story about this.

Over the last few years, it's become tradition for me and a bunch of my friends (women only) to go on a "mama's trip" to a gorgeous place somewhere in the world, preferably somewhere that none of us has been to before.

The first trip was completely spontaneous. I was heading to Belgium in the coming few days to fetch my eldest son, who had just completed a student exchange. I thought it might be fun to take a friend along to make a bit of an adventure out of it, so I casually asked five of my friends if anyone would be available on such and such a date for a spontaneous girls' trip.

I was fully expecting them all to decline on account of work, prior commitments, or having young children at home, but I was pleasantly surprised when all of them jumped at the chance.

Being the pattern interrupter that I am, I suggested that we use the opportunity to do things in a way that we normally wouldn't. Why? Because it keeps us youthful, as I told them!

And so I booked our transportation: six tickets on Megabus, the bus service from London to Brussels. I'll never forget the look of horror on the face of one particular friend who was used to traveling everywhere on first-class trains or planes.

To be fair, none of us had traveled long distances on a bus since we were children, so the idea of it was quite daunting.

It turned out Fabulous!

We arrived early at the bus depot and made sure we were the first aboard to claim the best top-deck seats—right at the front—and while the bus ambled along, we laughed and chatted, ate and drank, and the hours raced by. It was so much fun and certainly more memorable than a car ride or train trip. From then on, we called ourselves the "Mega Mamas," and the Mega Mamas went on to have many more bus adventures—in Sweden, Italy, and Spain, and still counting.

Anyway, my story takes place on our trip to Sweden.

We were there in the summer, staying in a glorious little hut on one of the islands in the Stockholm archipelago. One glorious evening, we were enjoying our dinner alfresco, on the edge of a gorgeous lake, with the sound of water gently lapping at our feet.

We were having one of our deep and intimate conversations (it's amazing how many of those happen amongst a group of women away from home), and in a moment of vulnerability, I brought up how I sometimes struggle with being the odd one out, even amongst my dearest friends.

In response, my friend sitting next to me said she was surprised by that. She thought I was very much part of the group, and *she* was clearly the odd one out. Then the friend opposite piped up; this was news to her because she often felt that *she* didn't quite fit in.

> *It turned out that every single one of us in that group felt like we didn't quite belong, for whatever reason.*

Isn't it interesting the "stories" we tell ourselves and the view we have of ourselves that perhaps no one else shares? More about stories later.

Despite having an unconventional view of the world, my adult years were nothing unconventional. Before *Fabulous* (BF), I had two core career iterations. The first was as the founder and CEO of a boutique public relations agency in South Africa, where I worked with premium brands in the beer, cigarette, and aviation industries. This was ironic because I've never smoked and don't drink much!

The second was as a full-time home-based mom-student, raising four kids and studying in between.

Also during that time, I immigrated twice, lost my parents to illness, discovered a new older sister on my mother's side, fought depression, lost money, made money, built friendships, lost friendships, had a miscarriage, was held up at gun-point in my own home, experienced an empty nest, and started perimenopause. Nothing special or out of the ordinary. I'm just like you, living life with all its delicious ups and downs, challenges, and joys.

Fabulosity came into my life unexpectedly, but it was influenced by four key decision points early on in my life that I'll share with you.

How Are You, Bruce?

Bruce (whose name has been changed) was a fellow in my high school class.

He was a highly intelligent go-getter but a terrible student who flunked most of his lessons because he was bored. He really couldn't understand the point of school, and he wanted to get out into the big, wide world and make money. He was a very likable, charismatic guy who led his fellow students into all sorts of mischief.

My overriding memory of Bruce is that whenever you asked him how he was, he would answer something along the lines of:

I'm so fantastic, it's frightening.

This type of language is pretty much unheard of in a teenage boy, and every time I heard it, it was still surprising.

To this day, what I remember about those words is how they made me *feel.*

The boldness, positivity, and expansive energy of those words were scintillating and contagious, making me feel like I was also frighteningly fantastic.

Through this experience with Bruce, I understood the power of assertive, optimistic, and audacious language and decided to also use more compelling, uplifting, and *Fabulous* words whenever I could.

The Torment Of The Bus

Fast forward a few years. At this time, I was in college, still introverted, and somewhat goody-goody.

Every day I would catch the bus to my campus, and every day I would go through the excruciating ordeal of standing at the bus stop waiting for number 15 to arrive. There was no reason for my high anxiety levels, yet they were sky high. What I was scared of, I have no idea.

When the bus would eventually arrive, I would climb aboard and, as quickly as possible, scoot into the first available seat. I would then breathe a sigh of relief that my morning bus ordeal was over while dreading the afternoon return journey.

But that's not all.

Every day during college lunchtime, I would walk past the canteen, looking wistfully through the window at all the students having a great time. I really wanted to go in, but it was just too intimidating. What I was scared of, I have no idea.

However, one day, it all changed.

On this particular day, while waiting for the morning bus with the usual knot in my stomach and feelings of dread, something inside me snapped. And out of the blue, I said to myself (and I remember the exact words):

This is not the way to go through life.

I decided there and then to just stop being scared of everything for no reason. When the bus arrived, I climbed aboard and steadfastly forced myself to walk all the way to the back, scanning from left to right, pretending to look for the best seat, just like other people do.

> I turned around, forced myself to
> walk all the way to the front again,
> chose my seat, and sat down.

OMG. I still remember that feeling of absolute triumph. I was the queen of the world with my newfound courage!

That same lunchtime, I sort of frogmarched myself into the college canteen. I bought a salad roll (even though I had a sandwich in my bag), looked for a table to sit at, and munched away while I nonchalantly paged through my notebook, looking up periodically and pretending that I was relaxed and casual, just like everyone else.

After what felt like eons but was in reality only a few minutes, I packed up and walked out, again feeling like I just conquered Mount Everest.

I felt so deliciously bold and courageous.

The decision that I no longer wanted to live as a shy, fearful mouse changed the trajectory of my life in such an incredible way. One decision!

Going forward, that year of college was a time of phenomenal personal growth for me. I applied to the Student Representative Council, where I had to campaign for votes! In front of REAL students! That took courage, but I did it!

I entered the college beauty pageant (and, to my great surprise, won) and was thrown into press interviews, photocalls, and social events.

As the reigning queen, I was obliged to organize the same pageant for the following year, requiring me to step completely out of my comfort zone to deal with budgets, sponsors, graphic designers, technical people, and more.

It was the most wonderful year of discomfort and excitement, and I loved it, all because of one expansive decision to change my life.

No More Depression, Thank You

Fast forward 15 years, and at this stage, I'm a wife and mom to four children, living with my family in Belgium after emigrating from South Africa six months earlier.

Although it was a conscious choice to emigrate and felt so exciting to begin with, I found the adjustment to our new country very difficult.

Our finances had taken a knock. We said goodbye to family, *adios* to dear friends, and closed the doors to a home by the sea that we loved.

We had to start from scratch and find a place for ourselves in a brand new community of strangers. Suddenly, the cumulation of all the goodbyes, feelings of loss, and new challenges of starting again became a heavy cross to bear.

All of this was happening below the surface of what appeared to be an idyllic life.

My husband, Mark, is a rock, and he held us in so many ways through this time. Having promised us a "super new home in a forest," he set about manifesting exactly that, deep in the heart of a little hilltop wood near Leuven, a gorgeous medieval university city in Belgium.

We placed our kids in the local Flemish Steiner school and watched them go from zero to fluent Flemish in just three short months. I make it sound painless; it wasn't. The kids found the initial language barrier very frustrating but looking back, they think it was well worth it. They are so grateful for both the experience, and the life-long ability to speak another language.

We also met some great people and made friends easily. We loved growing our social network, and we lived a rich life, often exploring the surroundings and traveling to many other European countries on weekends and during holidays.

Yet still, my low mood continued lurking below the surface, and I couldn't shake it off. I didn't like feeling down, which made me feel even worse.

One day, I woke up feeling sick and tired of melancholy. I decided enough was enough.

I remembered the "day of the bus" many years prior when I made the decision to change my life, and I knew I needed a similar pivotal moment.

There and then, I decided two things:

> 1. I don't want my kids to grow up with a depressed mother, and

> 2. I want nothing less than to look *Fabulous*, feel *Fabulous*, and do *Fabulous* things.

This is easier said than done when you're feeling the opposite, so I committed to starting small, and undertaking a process of what I now call "*Fabification*".

Fabification is where you constantly upgrade or "*Fabify*" everything you think, say, or do; in other words, you make small improvements and, where possible, build on them every day.

So, for example, I *Fabified* my breakfast. Instead of slugging back some coffee on the morning school run, I chose a healthier option like fruit and yogurt.

The next day, I ate out of a beautiful bowl instead of the first clean container to come out of the dishwasher.

The following day, I intentionally sat at the kitchen table to eat my breakfast, enjoying the morning sun. The day after that, I followed the meal with a 10-minute walk in the fresh air.

I *Fabified* my mindset. Whenever I found myself thinking negative thoughts or slipping into feeling sorry for myself, I stopped in my tracks, making myself unavailable for anything other than *Fabulous* thoughts. I forced myself to think positively, and if necessary, I would walk into another room.

In this way, I served as my own pattern interrupter and forced myself to swap negative patterns for positive ones.

Some days this was easier to do than other days, but the more I practiced focusing on *Fabulous*, the easier it became.

I also Fabified my words.

Thinking back to my friend Bruce and how his rousing words had a direct impact on how expansive I felt, I started to use juicier, bigger, bolder language, really feeling the energy of words.

This alone brought incredible bursts of feelings of well-being and excitement, even though there was nothing new or tangible to be excited about.

Every day I made sure that I *Fabified* something, no matter how small, keeping up with the *Fabifications* I had already introduced the day before. Some days I managed more *Fabifications* than others, and I let myself off the hook if things didn't quite work out the way I set out for the day.

This simple process of *Fabification* was awesome.

My depression lifted.

I started to enjoy the process of thinking about what could be *Fabified* every day and found myself feeling more positive about life in general.

I started getting out more, which helped me create new and adventurous behavior patterns.

I made some great friends, and together we had lots of fun, making the most of what life had to offer.

Due to my lighter mood, the atmosphere in the house improved. I became a more patient mother and a better wife.

My energy and vitality increased.

By focusing on expansion and micro-improvements, I spent more and more time
  looking,
    feeling,
      and
        doing
          Fabulous.

What I didn't realize at the time was that Fabification was forcing me to live in the present.

And the present is the place where happiness resides. I'll say more about that later.

Just at the time I was starting to feel better and just as we started to settle in our new country, we decided we wanted to begin another geographical adventure! I must be a sucker for punishment!

This time we had a move to the UK on our radar, as we wanted to give our kids the chance to connect with their British roots and spend some time with their English grandparents. We also wanted them to feel like global citizens, having the confidence to live anywhere in the world.

Again, another upheaval with many mixed emotions as we packed up, said goodbye to the wonderful people we befriended in Belgium, and relocated to Devon, UK.

But this time around, we had some international relocation experience, so settling in was much easier, and we quickly integrated into our new community.

Daily life looked much the same as in Belgium, and I continued to enjoy my roles as mother, wife, and self-student.

I had a thirst for learning, particularly about branding, design, entrepreneurship, style, self-confidence and midlife issues, and I became a course junkie on these subjects, learning from all the best mentors and trainers on the internet.

I also started helping women with style, confidence, and website design, and tried my hand at retail by launching two home-based products to sell at markets and local shops.

This was all in preparation for a potential new career when I eventually emerged from motherhood. Although I loved my previous career in PR, I wanted to do something new and exciting, but I didn't know what.

Before I knew it, 15 years had gone by, the kids had grown into teenagers, and they were making plans to study away from home. I found myself uttering the words, "Where did the time go?" and suddenly I was in the cliches of "the next chapter" and an "emptying nest."

WTF?

> *The emptying nest was a big milestone for me for the obvious reasons that the kids were leaving home and I was entering a new chapter and identity.*

But it also brought back memories of the unexpected trauma I myself experienced when I left home almost 30 years earlier. I'll never forget that day, and I need to share it for you to understand where *Fabulosity* came from.

Moving Out

For background, I've always had a complex relationship with my mother, who is now deceased.

We were close on one level, and she was a great mom to my two sisters and me. She did not have an easy childhood herself (I would say she was never "seen" by her socialite parents, and her emotional needs were seldom met). Her adult life was also no walk in the park, with two divorces, financial difficulties, depression, and some other really traumatic stuff that no one should ever go through.

Despite her troubled history, she and my father provided us with a loving home, and my childhood was happy on the whole. I say "on the whole" because my father struggled to cope with our financial challenges and used alcohol to relax and escape. Every so often, he would drink way beyond his limit, and he would become someone akin to a ranting despot.

I remember many evenings having to sit through tirades where he would shout and stomp, blaming my mom and the world for all his troubles. It never turned to violence, but it was very scary watching my dad, who was a loving man when sober, become someone else in his inebriation.

My mom handled these scenes very calmly, constantly reassuring us that Dad was just venting and would be back to his old self the next morning. And that, indeed, was always the case.

My dad was an affable family-oriented man at heart, and he was very proud of his children. He was an uncomplicated man who worked hard, and enjoyed the simple things in life, like a hot meal in the evenings, reading his newspaper, and watching boxing on TV.

So despite intermittent unpleasant alcoholic outbursts from my dad, my sisters and I were loved and looked after, living our lives and filling our days with school, dancing recitals, and swimming in our garden pool through the long and glorious South African summers.

My mom really enjoyed mothering young girls, and she was very present with us, both physically and emotionally.

She spent much of her time playing taxi to and from school and dance class, and she had endless patience sewing costumes and helping us polish our performances.

She was a great confidante, helping us navigate the ups and downs of growing up with a patient, listening ear, sound advice, and a loving embrace when needed.

My mom was also protective and honest, always encouraging us to do our best and developing our self-confidence. Motherhood gave her life purpose and meaning, so while we were young, she felt very secure and content in her role.

Our teenage years were more of a struggle for her. She found it difficult that we were using the wings she gave us, and she was often disgruntled when we went out with friends or made plans that didn't include her.

> I found this very confusing.
> When I left school and started college,
> the world was suddenly opening to me,
> and I was loving the opportunities that
> were coming my way since I no longer
> allowed shyness to hold me back.
> On the surface, my mom was happy to
> see me grow in confidence and independence,
> but deep down inside, I think she had
> a terrible fear of abandonment.

After I graduated college, I moved into the world of work and joined an international public relations agency. I loved both the PR industry and being an up-and-coming career woman. I had great relationships with my colleagues and clients, and it was an exciting time, with me learning and growing every day.

This was also where I met my now-husband of 27 years, Mark. Things moved quite quickly in our relationship, and after a year of dating, we knew we were meant for each other and decided that I would finally leave home and move in with him.

The problem was that, during this time, my mother's relationship with my dad had reached a boiling point.

> Although I was still living at home,
> I didn't spend much time there,
> so I wasn't really aware of the
> day-to-day drama of their relationship.

One day I arrived home from work to the news that my dad had left. On one level, it wasn't really a surprise for me or my mom, but it was still a shock.

This new situation presented me with a dilemma. I wanted to be a support to my mom through this tough time, but at the age of 24, I was beyond ready to leave home, and it was time for me to stand on my own two feet. I also reasoned that staying at home wasn't going to help her much, plus I was only moving 45 minutes away.

After some thought, I decided there was not much point in delaying moving out, so a couple of days later, with many mixed emotions, I packed my few belongings.

As I prepared to say good-bye to my mom as I took my first tentative steps into adulthood, she slapped me.

My mother slapped me.

I was so shocked. This was my mom, a head shorter than me, angry as a snake, but who had never lifted a finger to me before. Of course, being a clueless young adult, I was outraged to be treated so badly by my mother. I mean, she should have been happy for me, right?

Now that I'm an adult and a parent myself, I can understand the magnitude of the moment when your first child leaves home, particularly under horrible personal circumstances and I now realize that her anger was a disguise for fear and loss, and I forgive my mom for being human.

> With hindsight, I could have been
> less self-centred and waited a few
> months before I left so she wouldn't
> feel the loss so much. Waiting would
> have served both of us better because,
> the way it played out, I was too concerned
> about my mother's emotional pain
> to have any space to acknowledge
> this milestone moment for myself.

I put all my own emotions aside at the time, and this big event passed without celebration.

Little did I know that this little scene—where I'm moving away and leaving my grieving mom behind—would play out again in the future, not once over the years, but three times!

Mark and I (and luckily our children too) all enjoy change, which has prompted us to move towns, cities, and continents over time for pure adventure reasons, causing a great deal of anguish for my mom as we moved further and further away.

> *I've had to work hard over a fairly long period of time to deal with the guilt of "abandoning" her, even though I knew on an intellectual level that I was not actually abandoning her and had nothing to feel guilty about.*

The point of this story is to tell you that then and there I made a commitment to myself that, if I could help it, I would never put my future children in the same position.

> *I would do all I could to reinvent myself often and to create my own full, independent life, allowing them the freedom and space to fly the nest knowing that I would be ok without them.*

I vowed they would never need to feel guilty for living their lives to the fullest. Or for experiencing what the whole world has to offer. I wanted them to know that my life and happiness were not their responsibility.

So, although I was very far from an empty nest at that stage and didn't have any children yet, I realized then that the mindset work for this goal should begin immediately. Talk about planning ahead!

But I needed the right role models.

Where does one begin finding some? I asked myself.

Wanted: Role Models

I asked the Universe, and the Universe responded. My search for role models yielded two fantastic results. One came in the form of my in-laws-to-be!

Mark comes from a stoic British family. His father was a commander and helicopter test pilot in the Navy; his mother was a homemaker, church warden, and all sorts of other things.

She gave up a full-time career when she married and often jokes that she was always way too busy to work anyhow.

My in-laws have the view that bringing children into the world is a selfish act, and thus there is no contract between child and parent.

They believe it is incumbent on parents to create a welcoming, fun environment so that children want to be around them, but there is never any obligation for the children to visit them, live near them, support them in any way, or even be part of their lives.

They love being witnesses to their children's experiences of life and participate wherever they can in the spirit of independence and equality, but there is never any expectation.

When Mark left the UK as a young man to live in South Africa, there was no feeling that he was abandoning his family. Were his parents immune to feeling the loss? I'm sure they weren't, but they coped with it well because they embodied the ethos of Khalil Gibran, who so eloquently said:

> "Your children are not your children.
> They are the sons and daughters
> of life's longing for itself.
> They come through you but not from you,
> and though they are with you,
> they belong not to you."

This point of view really resonates with me, and has helped me make peace with that strange day many years ago. It's also helping me cope with my own empty nest now.

The second role model came in the form of Ari Seth Cohen and his Advanced Style movement.

Advanced Style is a project devoted

> "to capturing the sartorial savvy
> of the senior set."

On his website, Ari says: *"I feature people who live full, creative lives. They live life to the fullest, age gracefully, and continue to grow and challenge themselves."*

OMG. Seeing the photographs he publishes of women (and men) in their seventies and eighties, looking *Fabulous* in bright, outlandish outfits, going out together, having fun, and being seen—it turned me on BIG TIME!

I knew that *joie de vivre* and "fabulosity" (in the dictionary, defined as 'the state of being fabulous'), were the keys to happiness at any age, and I wanted some!

The Story So Far

So now you see that there were various pivotal moments in my life that paved the way for the word "*Fabulous*" to become my anchor and life philosophy.

I'm also forever grateful to my positive octogenarian role models, who showed me that life is for living in spectacular fashion, without guilt or reliance on anyone else for happiness.

Let's disembark from the time machine and return to the more recent point where my habit of *Fabification* was really starting to take off and *Fabulosity* was just beginning to become a "thing".

PART II

YOU CREATE WHAT YOU THINK YOU ARE

Hello Queen Of Fabulosity

I was interviewed on a podcast the other day by a delightful fifty-something podcaster.

She was fascinated by the whole concept of *Fabulosity* which is, for most people, a way of thinking about life that is somewhat more flamboyant and outlandish than they're used to. I get it.

Towards the end of the podcast, she asked who first named me the Queen of *Fabulosity*. When I told her it was me, her eyes went wide.

You might also be surprised by this but if not me, who?

I'm the one in charge of building my self-identity—no one else is.

It's funny how society contradicts itself. We're supposed to aspire to develop internal validation, and yet we're very quickly judged to be boastful or arrogant if we "toot our own horn." There's a disconnect somewhere, don't you agree?

Through the *Fabulosity* process, I've realized that very few people have an expansive mindset, whether it's for themselves or for others. To call yourself "fabulous" is, for too many people, a step too far. I want to change that!

But I'm getting ahead of myself with this story. I need to first explain how this title came about in the first place!

By now, *Fabification* was a daily habit, and it was not only lifting me out of my low mood and home sickness after we emigrated to Belgium. It was starting to ignite something else inside of me.

It was making me want to look, feel, do, and be MORE … more *Fabulous*, Sensational, Awesome, Incredible—all the big, juicy words! I had a yearning desire to expand outside of my comfort zone and explore my wings.

But how far could I take this *Fabulosity* thing? Just how *Fabulous* could I look, feel, do and be?

I began to really fall in love with the energy, expansiveness, and possibility of this exciting "F" word, and I began to dream about what it would mean to take it to its extreme in my life. That's when I realized I had to become the person for whom looking, feeling, doing and being *Fabulous* were easy.

I had to become the "Queen of Fabulosity."

The thoughts and emotions I experienced in the few seconds that followed were very interesting.

First, I felt utter exhilaration. I felt so godlike, gigantic, and euphoric (aren't these great words?) at the thought of it, and I felt like I'd just birthed the next Lady Gaga!

In the next split second, I thought about how cringeworthy and crazy it was. Stupid idea. Childish. I'll make a fool of myself. This is far too outlandish and silly.

But maybe that's not true. It's outlandish, sure, but it's also titillating and inspirational. It makes me feel like I can achieve anything.

No. Don't be silly. It's too big for me. I'm just little old me. I can't be so arrogant.

And so it went on, round and round in circles in my head, until eventually my competitive spirit took over and I thought, "You don't think I can be the Queen of *Fabulosity*? Just watch me!"

So, I challenged myself to try it out and see where it went.

I didn't tell anyone about this sensational persona I had just created for myself. It was MY delicious secret, and I just enjoyed the fire and daring of seeing the world through the eyes of the Queen of *Fabulosity*.

It was like a secret power that only I possessed.

To become her, I had to find answers to some compelling questions.

What would she wear?
How would she stand?
What would she eat?
How would she talk to people?
How would she walk into a room?
How would she tackle challenges and
 disappointments?

And then some deeper questions.

How does she feel about aging?
What does she stand for?
Who is she?
What impact does she have on people?
The world?

It was a fascinating, delightful, and sometimes painful process of introspection, dreaming, and self-expression in ways that had never occurred to me before.

I had never asked myself what my point of view was. Or what I stood for. Or what difference I wanted to make.

For the next few months, I continued the process of self-exploration while at the same time living life as the Queen of *Fabulosity*.

I was having such fun with it, and one day it occurred to me:

> *I would love to support other women to become their own Queens of Fabulosity and find their version of Fabulous too.*

And so began my journey as the Chief Instigator of the *Fabulosity* movement.

When I started to delve into why such a seemingly silly title like the Queen of *Fabulosity* could be so powerful, I started to uncover some incredible insights spawned by people much more knowledgeable than I. Grab a coffee in a gorgeous cup, and let's explore some of these insights next.

Self-Identity Is Everything

"Self-identity is everything" are my words, but the sentiment is based on various psychologists and theorists who espouse that we act in alignment with who we think we are.

And in the words of the incredible Tony Robbins: "The strongest force in the human personality is the need to stay consistent in how we define ourselves."

Unfortunately, this is true whether you have a positive or negative self-identity.

And, unfortunately, negative self-identity is rife.

So often, incredible, intelligent women cannot see their beauty, wisdom, and value, and so they either shrink and hide, or live without fully sharing their gifts with the world.

If a woman defines herself as a bland, washed-out housewife with no prospects, that's exactly how she'll show up, and that's exactly the result she'll create for herself.

On the other hand, if a woman decides she is a *Fabulous*, vibrant, slim woman—even if she is carrying extra weight—guess what? She will behave, dress, and eat like a *Fabulous*, vibrant, slim woman, loving her life and probably losing weight without trying too.

Self-Identity Is A Habit

In my experience, the good and bad news about self-identity is that, like most things, it's a habit. Yes, of course, self-identity is affected by other factors like culture, experiences, beliefs, values, and so on, but I like to believe that these "defaults" can all be overridden by habits.

In the example above, the woman in question is in the habit of believing what she believes about herself. And this results in her finding evidence to support her beliefs. The more evidence she finds, the more she believes it, and the more she becomes what she believes.

My point is that, in my experience, we don't need to give in to our defaults of culture, family history, and past experiences.

> *Our self-identity can change if we just get into the habit of creating a new one, even if we fake it in the beginning.*

Another slightly obscure way of putting it is that we start to believe anything if we are told it long enough (this is why gaslighting is so destructive), and we can even start to believe our own lies!

This brings up a lovely story about my sister, who, as a teenager, used to regularly lie to my mother about her whereabouts.

At some point, my mother cottoned on to her and called her bluff. My sister was absolutely outraged that my mother did not believe her until her best friend reminded her that she was, in fact, not telling the truth. She had become so accustomed to her own lies that she believed them herself.

> *When I got into the habit of my new self-identity, the Queen of Fabulosity, it became easier and easier to think like her and be her, even when I didn't really believe it in the beginning!*

I'm not sure what the general consensus is about how long it takes to develop new habits; all I know is that it's taken me a remarkably short time to develop the Queen of *Fabulosity* habit.

Am I perfect at it? No. Of course, there are bad days where I feel the opposite, but I definitely bounce back quicker and don't take life as seriously as I did before.

Be, Do, Have

One of my mentors is a very down-to-earth, straight-talking life coach named Jim Fortin. He first introduced me to the concept of the Be-Do-Have model of success, which I just love!

In a nutshell, the Be-Do-Have model says that self-identity (Be) is fundamental to success, and that Be should always be first, with the other words following in that order. In other words, we should focus on becoming the person we need to be (Be) to take the action required (Do) to achieve the outcome we want (Have).

> *The common mistake most people make is that they get the order wrong.*

They follow the "Have-Do-Be" model, where they believe they must first accumulate more knowledge, wealth, resources, or experiences (Have) to then do what they must do (Do) to become the person they want to be (Be). This doesn't work, and they get stuck.

Or they follow "Do-Have-Be," where they simply work all the time (Do), thinking this will lead to the resources they need (Have), which will then make them who they want to be (Be). This is usually not sustainable because whatever "resources" they have are never enough. So they never reach their goal. How awful is that?

Everything Is A Story

I have no idea where I came across the notion that "*everything* is a story", but for me, it's been a game changer.

The crux of this idea is that all our beliefs—the negative as well as the positive ones—are merely interpretations, not facts.

All the "too"s, whether *positive* or negative, are just stories:

I'm too old. I'm too fat. I'm too thin. I'm too young. I'm too beautiful. I'm too ugly. I'm too stupid. I'm too clever.

Our "shortcomings" and "positive attributes" are stories too:

I don't have enough experience. I have nothing to contribute. I'm irreplaceable. I don't add any value. I add great value. I'm great at math. I'm bad at math.

The idea that "there are no facts, only interpretation" was written about by the German philosopher Friedrich Nietzsche in the 1800s, and it's said to have had a profound influence on many fields, including philosophy, psychology, and literary theory.

I'm playing with this idea as an experiment in my own life, and it's very interesting to me because there are so many thoughts, usually negative and unhelpful ones, that I interpret as facts but which are actually just stories.

Now that I'm more conscious of this, when a negative thought comes up, I usually quickly realize that it's a self-limiting belief or story that I can change to one that better supports me in my pursuit of looking, feeling, doing and being *Fabulous*.

Am I really the Queen of *Fabulosity*? Who's to say, but it's an appealing story that makes me happier than the Queen of Failure or the Doyenne of Doom and Gloom, that's for sure!

Here's another perspective I'd like to share with you...

Insights From A Plastic Surgeon

At the time of writing, I'm slightly distracted by another book I've just found called *Psycho-Cybernetics* by Maxwell Maltz, a plastic surgeon.

I'm ignoring all temptation to dip into it instead of writing this chapter because anyone who's written a book will know that you get to a stage where resistance kicks in and everything else seems more urgent, important, and enticing than actually finishing writing the book!

Anyhow, I digress.

I read just enough of the introductory pages to get me excited, but I wanted to share this juicy tidbit from the first few paragraphs that fits in with exactly what we're talking about.

> "When a facial disfigurement is corrected by plastic surgery, dramatic psychological changes result ONLY IF there is a corresponding correction of the mutilated self-image. Sometimes the image of a disfigured self persists even after successful surgery, much the same as the phantom limb may continue to feel pain years after the physical arm or leg has been amputated."

In simple terms, the only time plastic surgery can make you feel better about yourself is if you have a positive self-image.

Your Self-image (or self-identity) really is everything. It's the place from which all good and bad things stem. Every day I prioritize my self-identity, and I try to choose my stories carefully.

If you want a healthy self-identity, create habits that support who you want to be, and if you don't like the self-identity you've created (consciously or unconsciously), guess what? You can change it!

Let's talk more about how to go about that in the *Fabosphere*.

I'd like to introduce you to two concepts that we talk about a lot. The one is *reinvention* (which I'll go into later), and the other, which I'll talk about first, is the concept of You 2.0.

You 2.0

For anyone who is unfamiliar with the "2.0" reference, the first public version of any product or software is called "1.0."

After that, the new and improved version is called 2.0, and it usually represents a major leap forward based on the experience and learning of 1.0.

Version 2.0 cannot exist without version 1.0, and version 1.0 only exists to be improved, without shame, guilt, or embarrassment.

When you step into your *Fabulosity*, you start on the path of unleashing You 2.0—the significantly enhanced and improved version of the original you. This iteration is built on the *Fabulous* question: "Who would you like to be next?"

Disclaimer

I'm not saying there's anything wrong with the current version of you, but I think you're reading this book because, like me, you want MORE, and you're ready to expand into the fullest, most exciting version of yourself.

Unfortunately, most women don't have a clue about who they would like to be.

We are simply not in the habit of confronting ourselves in this way, perhaps because the world seems to be obsessed with "authenticity" and "being who you are."

Yes, I agree that knowing who you are is very important, but to me, it feels limiting and leaves little scope or imagination for self expansion.

Ironically, in my own life, asking the question "Who do I want to be next?" helped me to really find myself by uncovering unexplored facets that I had no idea were there. I know it sounds contradictory so let me illustrate:

> I'm writing this book because my answer to that question was that I wanted to be an author.
>
> I started my podcast because I wanted to be a podcaster.
>
> I started the *Fabulosity* work when I decided to be bold, brave, and *Fabulous*.

None of these things were on my radar in the past, but they are very much part of who I am today because I identified who I wanted to be, and started behaving like that person.

I'm not a psychology buff, but to me, it makes sense that if you desire to be someone or something else, it's actually already a part of you that wants to come out.

Perhaps that's why personas are so powerful. They allow you to step outside of your conscious self and try on an identity that could be a part of you that you may not know is there.

Clothes can have that same effect. Actors find it so much easier to embody their roles once they have on their costumes and make-up.

And there is no bride in the world who can be upstaged on her wedding day because she is indisputably the star of the show.

Why?

Because she totally embodies that role for the day, supported by her outfit and all the other elements that create the sense of occasion that every wedding day has.

So, who do YOU want to be next?

I believe women who give themselves the time and freedom to explore this question will discover that it's a magical exercise, that will yield unexpected, surprising, and delightful results that will, in fact, take them closer to their true selves.

Like anything, we can make this as simple or as hard as we like, but since I like simplicity, I've listed some questions that can get the process started. You'll recognize some of these from earlier because I went through this process to become the Queen of *Fabulosity*.

Keep these questions in the back of your mind while you read this book, and then come back to them in earnest afterward. It will be much more satisfying and potent to develop You 2.0 when you're in a *Fabulous* mindset, so be patient.

Here are the questions:

What does You 2.0 look like?
Who is the boldest, most confident, most expansive version of you?
What are her favorite words?
How does she show up?
What does she like?
What doesn't she like?
What is she no longer available for?
How does she make people feel?
How does she act?
How does she deal with obstacles?

How does she react to negative comments?
What does she stand for?
What topics are close to her heart?
What change in the world does she want to be part of?
What's her purpose or mission at this stage of her life?
What happened in her past that made her who she is today?

And if other questions come up, answer those too. Let it all flow out of you. If it's a struggle, relax! It will come in its own time. Read the rest of this book first, then come back to these questions and keep tuning into yourself.

Once you have a starting idea of what You 2.0 could look like, the work is to start embodying her, beginning right now, in the smallest, biggest, or messiest way possible. It doesn't have to be perfect, as long as you start to move in the direction of her, and you start where you are.

> *This is such a powerful idea that it can honestly change how you think about yourself and, thus, what's possible for you.*

Even if you don't believe you can, just pretend you're an actress playing a role in a movie. Put on the role of You 2.0 like a bejeweled cloak, and just start. It doesn't matter if you do it badly to begin with; keep improving every day. Don't think; just do.

> Perfection kills a lot of dreams, just like procrastination and overthinking.
> PLUS
> the Universe rewards action, not thought.

Start to act like she would. Use the language that she would use. Exude the confidence that she would exude, even if you don't feel it to begin with.

Become her, and have some fun with it! You don't need to tell anyone.

It can be your delicious little secret if you choose.

As you go through this book, you'll find inspiration and new perspectives that will help you shape You 2.0, so at this stage, keep an open mind and just enjoy the exploration and anticipation.

The Story So Far

How you see yourself determines everything.

To achieve what you want, you first have to become a person worthy of it.

What you think of yourself is a story, and this story can be changed at any time, regardless of how it became a story in the first place.

Your story is a habit.

Who do you want to be next? Start to act, think, and behave like You 2.0, the new and expanded version of you.

PART III

WHEN YOU CHOOSE FABULOUS, FABULOUS CHOOSES YOU

Introducing... Fabulosity

We're finally at the point of the book where I can dive into my actual definition of *Fabulosity* and unpack it so it hopefully makes sense and instills in you a desire to make it your default software program!

"Fabulosity", as previously mentioned, is a derivative of the word "fabulous", and just like "fabulicious", surprisingly, it's in the dictionary.

My version is so much more than

"the state of being fabulous,"

...and has evolved into a habit and life philosophy that, in a nutshell, inspires and empowers women to live with more freedom, fun, and audacity.

Here's the full definition of my version, and then I'll break it down.

> *Fabulosity is the habit of*
> *embracing, loving, and trusting all aspects of*
> *yourself (good, bad, and ugly) and all aspects*
> *of your life (past, present, and future)*
> *so that fear is reduced,*
> *courage is enhanced*
> *and you can fully express yourself*
> *to live life as an experiment*
> *with lightness, curiosity, and*
> *a sense of adventure.*

Life is either a daring adventure.
Or it's nothing.

Helen Keller

Fabulosity
is the HABIT of
embracing, **loving,** and *trusting*
all aspects of YOURSELF
(good, bad, and ugly)
and
all aspects of your life
(past, present, and future)
so that *fear is reduced,*
courage is ENHANCED
and you can
fully express yourself
to *live life* as an EXPERIMENT with
lightness,
curiosity,
and
a SENSE *of* ADVENTURE

Habit

First and foremost, *Fabulosity* is a habit, not an art or a science, and it requires NO special skills, talents, circumstances, or looks.

It comes about through repetition and practice, and what a delightful thing to have on your calendar!

Embrace, Love And Trust

I love the word "embrace," which means "accept willingly and enthusiastically." It's such a great word and concept.

In *Fabulosity*, the goal is to embrace all aspects of yourself—the good, the bad, and the ugly.

Once you can embrace them, the next steps are to expand into the *Fabulous* by "loving" and "trusting" them too.

Fabulosity
is the HABIT of
embracing, **loving,** and *trusting*
all aspects of YOURSELF
(good, bad, and ugly)
and
all aspects of your life
(past, present, and future)
so that *fear is reduced,*
courage is ENHANCED
and you can
fully express yourself
to *live life* as an EXPERIMENT with
lightness,
curiosity,
and
a SENSE *of* ADVENTURE

Fabulous people embrace, love and trust all aspects of themselves—the good, bad, and ugly. Why the "good"? Surely everyone embraces the good in themselves?

One would think so, but in my experience, the world places much more emphasis on us improving our weaknesses than promoting our strengths.

Especially for women. We are taught to be humble and self-effacing, downplaying our virtues and talents so that we don't appear arrogant or conceited.

For many women, the "good" in them is invisible, or if they do see it, they view it as unimportant or "nothing."

If you ask any woman to make a list of her strengths and weaknesses, I'll bet you any amount that most women will have a short list of strengths and a long list of weaknesses.

The *Fabulous* work is to find out what we are good at and then embrace it. To love and trust it too. Can you imagine how powerful we would feel if we got to embrace, love, and trust our natural gifts and talents?

But what if you don't know what those are?

Don't worry. Most people don't. I invite you to explore some of these ideas:

ASK
Ask your closest family and friends this exact question: "What do you think my natural gifts are?" You'll be amazed at the lovely comments that come!

WRITE
Write down a list of things that you love to do; your gifts are often hidden among the answers.

CONTEMPLATE
Then, be honest about what you find to be the real reward for doing these things. For example: if you said "cooking for dinner parties", why do you like it? Do you like the showmanship/hosting part, or perhaps you love preparing your house and making the table arrangement? Perhaps you love the social aspect or you just love cooking.

LIST
Jot down a list of everything that people come to you for. Perhaps you're always helping people with their relationships. Or you're often being asked for business advice or recipes, or you're the first person people call upon in an emergency or to plan a party. Could these be clues?

REMINISCE
Think back to your childhood. What did you love to do or were good at? And the opposite? Sometimes it helps to think about what you didn't like to find what you did.

LOOK FOR CLUES
When you start looking for clues, you'll find them Have fun with this process, for which there is no deadline or end point. It's delicious, ongoing introspection that will yield some great insights into what you're good at. Once you have some ideas, start to look for patterns.

Of all the activities you seem to like and are good at, what do they all have in common? There is gold to be found if you are just intentional and mindful about exploring who you were, who you are, and then who you want to be.

OWN IT
Own it! Own it! Own it!   Own it! Own it! Embrace, love, and trust the hell out of these amazing skills, talents, and gifts that make you who you are. And also remember that you are always evolving, so this list will grow and change, especially if you subscribe to *Fabulosity*.

You're going to love yourself so much that you won't know what to do with yourself!

It's not only the "good" that needs embracing, loving, and trusting, but also the "bad" and the "ugly." These two aspects of ourselves (also known as the "shadow") are usually well known to us, but we tend to either want to hide them or wallow in them.

Fabulosity says the bad and the ugly are critical elements of our personalities and thus should be treated with love. They help to make us the incredible beings that we are.

If your shadows are keeping you stuck, and you find it impossible to even consider the idea that they are *Fabulous*, you might want to seek help from a professional. "Shadow work" is a powerful tool to work through this kind of stuff.
For the purposes of *Fabulosity*, we simply acknowledge and accept the shadow and focus on the work of looking forward, prioritizing positivity, and creating possibility.
We are not repressing anything in any way; in fact, we really encourage "negative" emotions to emerge and be acknowledged.

Spending short amounts of time feeling sad, angry, overwhelmed, anxious, upset, and all of these wonderfully human emotions is good for us.
Fabulosity says, Never waste a good crisis! When those feelings come, really feel them and give yourself time and space to cry, scream, punch the air, sleep, and watch movies—for an appropriate, limited amount of time only. That could be five minutes, a whole day, or a year, depending on the severity of its cause.
But, at the appropriate time, shift focus to the future, leave behind the past knowing that everything happens FOR us, and become open to the lessons.

Life is a rich tapestry of ups and downs, and they are all necessary for us to have the full mortal experience.

That said, don't suffer in silence. If you need help to overcome grief, get the best kind of help you can. Go into it with the idea that you want to heal as quickly as possible. If you're still going to therapy five years later, perhaps you need another therapist... I'm being slightly flippant here because I know people for whom therapy is a long-term crutch not a temporary support agent.

Fabulosity is a life philosophy that acknowledges the shadow but doesn't focus on it. We simply put our energy into moving forward with delicious anticipation for better days.

Fabulosity
is the HABIT of
embracing, **loving,** and *trusting*
all aspects of YOURSELF
(good, bad, and ugly)
and
all aspects of your life
(past, present, and future)
so that *fear is reduced,*
courage is ENHANCED
and you can
fully express yourself
to *live life* as an EXPERIMENT with
lightness,
curiosity,
and
a SENSE *of* ADVENTURE

Past

We all have stories from our past that make us happy, angry, sad, emotional, or [insert emotion here]. *Fabulosity* says, Let's embrace, love, and trust all that has happened.

Every event has shaped us, and every event is *Fabulous*. It's not good or bad; it's just *Fabulous*.

I love the Taoist parable about the Chinese farmer who experiences a series of events. The first is that his new horse runs away, and his neighbors all commiserate with him at his misfortune.

He simply remains indifferent, saying, "Who's to know if it's good or bad?" Later on, the horse returns, bringing with him another horse, which the farmer then gives to his son. The neighbors are delighted on his behalf, congratulating him on this happy turn of events. The farmer remains neutral, saying, "Who's to know if it's good or bad? "

Unfortunately, the son falls off the horse and breaks his leg, again attracting the empathy of the neighbors, who express that they can't believe the farmer's bad luck. The farmer again remains neutral. A few days later, the son is exempt from fighting in a war due to his broken leg. Is that good or bad? Who knows, right?

I'd like to *Fabify* this story even more and say that the farmer could answer: It's not good or bad, just *Fabulous*!

In the Fabosphere, there is no good or bad, only Fabulous.

We just don't know why certain things happen. As I mentioned earlier, I like to believe the story that life happens FOR us, not TO us.

This reframe changes everything, putting us in a mindset of growth, learning, and, more importantly, experiencing what life is offering us.

Why are we in this incarnation but to experience and grow?

Even though we might not like or understand why certain things are happening in our lives—good or bad—they MUST be happening for a reason.

While we're going through tough times, this might be difficult to accept, but what other "story" would you prefer to believe?

That you deserve the misery you're going through?
That life stinks, and then you die?
That you're an unlucky person who has been given a raw deal?
That you always attract bad stuff?

These are also stories, but ones that won't serve you if your goal is *Fabulosity*. Are they true? Are they not true? Who knows. All I know is that in my life, I'm no longer available for negative stories.

In the Fabosphere, there is also no success or failure—only Fabulous.

I love listening to Sara Blakely, founder of Spanx and multi-millionaire, who talks about how her dad used to encourage her to fail. Every day, he would ask her to report on what she tried and failed at, and if she had nothing to report, he was disappointed. His agenda was to normalize failure and encourage her to take risks. I love this parenting approach.

Fear of failure can be a huge obstacle to achieving our goals. It can make us doubt ourselves, or our decisions, and hold us back from stepping out of our comfort zones.

Can you imagine how much happier we all would be if failure were normalized, or, as in Fabulosity, eradicated?

It simply does not exist in the *Fabosphere*. There's only learning, experience, and adventure! Nothing is bad, good, successful, or failed. All outcomes are *Fabulous*.

Tony Robbins, one of the greatest life strategists of all time, always tells the story that he was born and brought up in very difficult circumstances, but he recognizes that these very circumstances shaped who he became. He says he would not be Tony Robbins without them.

So, in my interpretation, although he didn't find it easy to go through what he did, looking back, it was all *Fabulous* because all his experiences became building blocks for his future happiness and success.

> *How awesome would it be if we could view our whole past with fondness?*

You see, if we deem all of it *Fabulous*, then we can move on to the more important job of looking to the future, and expanding into it in spectacular fashion.

I understand that this is not always easy. I'm not dismissing any atrocities or painful experiences that you might have gone through.

I've had my share of trauma, disappointment, shame, guilt, loss and more—we all have. But in the past these experiences belong, and I, for one, will not be focusing on them. I acknowledge that the past exists only as thoughts, and I choose my thoughts as much as possible. I put my focus on where I am now and my future. I'm not repressing the past or denying it; I'm just diverting my attention.

If you're struggling with something that's happened to you, please do whatever you can to turn your open wounds into scabs and scars as quickly as possible so that you can work on finding the lessons in the events that happened to you.

> *When you can judge them all as Fabulous and look to your awesome future, then you really are free.*

Forgiveness

Recently, I had the opportunity to work with a highly talented spiritual guide for a day. During our time together, we dove deeply into my goals and what barriers were impeding my progress. We all have barriers to achieving our next levels and I find it a fascinating process to chip away at the emotional layers we all have.

My session was an amazing experience, and it felt like a real luxury to spend an entire day exploring and expanding what's possible. I highly recommend it!

One of the "aha" moments I had was that despite spending the last two years in the *Fabosphere* and focusing on the positive, deep inside myself there were some stubborn hurt and anger issues that just would not shift, and these were real obstacles to reaching my next level of *Fabulosity*.

> *I was holding onto stuff that happened to me years ago, and it was still causing me pain.*

The main issue was I needed to forgive not only others for their so-called "transgressions", but also myself for my own shortcomings, my perceived lack of progress (the joys of being a Type A personality), and my errors in judgment in the broad context of my life lived thus far.

Even though *Fabulosity* is my daily life philosophy, and my "story" is that everything is *Fabulous*—including shortcomings, lack of progress, and mistakes—we all have ongoing, uncomfortable work to do to release stubborn energies and thought patterns, and I'm always so pleased when I've taken the time to do that kind of potent work.

Through the process, I realized that, like most of us, I'm my own worst enemy, and I hold myself to ridiculously high standards.

We're quicker to overlook or forgive others than ourselves. Hmmmff. This is a very bad habit that we need to change forthwith. Forgiveness is a gift that we give ourselves. It sets us free and helps us move on.

People often say they "can't" forgive. What they mean is that they won't. Of course, we *can* forgive if we decide to and seek the help we need. And to lead a *Fabulous* life, we have to! So get on with the forgiveness, starting with yourself. Holding on to resentment is toxic. Forgive.

Present

There's much talk these days about mindfulness and the importance of "living in the present."

Eleonor Roosevelt said,

> "The present is a "gift," which is why it's called the "present."

I love this perspective.

The present is the only place where we can fully engage with our surroundings and thoroughly immerse ourselves in the experiences of our lives. We cannot think to the left (our past) or the right (our future) when we're in the *now*.

The present is where Fabification takes place and where happiness resides.

The present is where we physically get into action. When we get into action, we feel alive and at one with ourselves. The energy starts to flow, we get momentum, and magic starts to happen.

In pursuit of living fully in the present, I want to highlight the *Fabulous* concept of "feeling alive" or "coming alive." No one says it better than Howard Thurman in this quote, one of my favorites:

> "Do not ask what the world needs.
> Ask what makes you come alive, and go do that,
> because what the world needs is
> people who have come alive."

This is such a powerful idea, and even just thinking about "coming alive" instantly lifts your vibration. It's "living in the present" on steroids.

Coming alive does not happen by itself. Again, it's a habit. And a choice. No matter what your circumstances, you can choose to come alive and feel the delicious tingling of pure joy just because you're breathing.

You can turn it on like a switch whenever you want to. Just simply decide to feel alive. Feel the fire and the magic deep inside your belly. It's there for the taking.

And do yourself a favor. Stay away from your phone and social media as much as possible. In my opinion, social media is pure voyeurism and destroys the human spirit. It presents us with a world in which everyone else shapes who we are and what we feel. Freedom from screens makes it so much easier to come alive and step into our own version of *Fabulous*, without distraction.

Limit your scrolling and use social media for your own visibility and marketing.

Future

The definition of *Fabulosity* includes embracing, loving, and trusting the future too. This is important because when we read the news or even look around us at the day-to-day difficulties facing a lot of people, it's so easy to get sucked into despair for the future.

As a species, we are also facing big existential challenges like the climate catastrophe, which so desperately needs prioritizing if we want to avoid large-scale human tragedy.

Some say it's too late to fix; others say it's a hoax; and others say let's keep trying, knowing that we'll figure it out and face what we need to with courage, love, and hope.

Fabulosity subscribes to the latter, inviting us to live every day with contagious energy and spirit, remain optimistic, and do what we can in our corner of the world to help.

A friend of ours always says that the happiest people he knows are those who deeply believe they cannot fix big issues (like the climate catastrophe).

> *Their happiness comes from continuing to try anyway, focusing on loving life, swapping material pursuits for experiential ones, and investing in deep, joyful relationships with caring people.*

For me, there is always hope. No one can foresee the future, and anything can happen.

> *, We are all ONE decision/ thought/ action/day away from changing our lives, no matter our circumstances.*

It's great to remember this when we're going through personal challenges that feel insurmountable. This too shall pass, and anything is possible if we remain optimistic, choose nourishing stories, and get in the game.

In terms of climate issues, with the speed of technological advances, we just have no idea the extent of what's possible.

If you're spiritually inclined, you might argue that as humans, we're not able to see the big picture, and if we believe that life is happening FOR us, not TO us, then we can trust that everything is unfolding as it should.

Always.

No matter how dire a situation seems.

I always remind myself that everyone is on this planet for a human experience, and who is to say which experience is good or bad?

I choose to believe that every experience is *Fabulous*, and I will trust the same for our future.

Fabulosity
is the HABIT of
embracing, **loving,** and *trusting*
all aspects of YOURSELF
(good, bad, and ugly)
and
all aspects of your life
(past, present, and future)
so that ***fear is reduced,***
courage is ENHANCED
and you can
fully express yourself
to *live life* as an EXPERIMENT with
lightness,
curiosity,
and
a SENSE *of* ADVENTURE

Whenever I think of fear, worry, or anxiety, I think of the utterly gorgeous Newt Scamandar in "Fantastic Beasts and Where to Find Them," who said:

If you worry, you suffer twice.

Fear, worry, and anxiety are often our most frequent bedfellows, and although there are nuances in the definitions of all these words, for our purposes, I'll categorize them as the same thing.

I tend to be a worrier, and in unchecked moments, I can find myself dwelling on all sorts of things that I have no control over.

> *Fabulosity is a savior when this happens because it gets me back to a higher vibration, allowing me to separate what's beyond my control from what isn't.*

Fear is a large category, but I thought it would be interesting to see which of the most common fears can be kicked into touch if *Fabulosity* is your default operating system.

Fear of failure
In Fabulosity, failure doesn't exist anymore because everything that happens is *Fabulous* and life is an experiment. Next.

Fear of the unknown
The unknown is not scary anymore because nothing can go "wrong."
You'll view the unknown with lightness, curiosity, and a sense of adventure (more about that later).

Fear of death or dying
This is a trickier one, and we probably all have a fear of death on some level.
But I hope that if you live in *Fabulous* fashion, you'll be too busy loving your life to give this much thought.

Fear of rejection or judgment

If you love everything about yourself and your life, there is no rejection, only *Fabulous*. Everyone is entitled to their own point of view, and if someone is not on the same page as you, it doesn't matter.
You don't need anyone else's approval anymore.

Fear of loneliness

Your *Fabulous* approach to life means you will create a network of friends wherever you are and seek the company of people who vibrate at your high level. No one else matters.

Fear of public speaking

If you do any type of public speaking, loving everything about yourself, and treating your life as an experiment (more about this later) means you don't need to be afraid of rejection from the audience.

Whatever they think about you is *Fabulous*, and whatever the quality of your performance, that's *Fabulous* too. We all start where we are, seeking to explore new challenges and improve on current ones. Perfect doesn't exist.

Fear of change

What? *Fabulous* people love change.
Ok, this might be a tricky one for some people, but just work on it, okay? Remember that life is an unknown adventure, meant to be explored! Change is an essential part of living a rich, memorable life.

Fear of failure to meet expectations

Not in this lifetime. If you love and trust all aspects of yourself, and everything is *Fabulous*, you won't worry about expectations anymore. Life is an experiment, which means expectations are eradicated. And in a world where expectations cause so much misery, good riddance.

Fear of losing control
Nope. When you live in the *Fabosphere* you don't worry about this because being "in control" is a story. We are not really in control of anything so let's remove this idea from our consciousness and just LIVE our delicious, exciting experiment.

Fear of being vulnerable
Not any more.
You can only be vulnerable if you have a fear of failure and judgement, which don't exist in the *Fabosphere*.

Fear of success
This is an insidious fear that some, if not most of us, suffer from without even knowing it. *Fabulosity* helps us to develop into the type of person that we must become to never suffer from this again!

Fear is a huge subject, but for the purposes of *Fabulosity*, all we want is to be conscious of how much of it relates to the unknown and failure.

If we can accept the *Fabulous* principle that everything we are and everything we do is *Fabulous*, fear becomes more manageable, and then, as we'll see in the next chapter, we create the possibility for courage to show up.

Fabulosity
is the HABIT of
embracing, **loving,** and *trusting*
all aspects of YOURSELF
(good, bad, and ugly)
and
all aspects of your life
(past, present, and future)
so that *fear is reduced,*
courage is ENHANCED
and you can
fully express yourself
to *live life* as an EXPERIMENT with
lightness,
curiosity,
and
a SENSE *of* ADVENTURE

In the *Fabulosity* definition, when fear is reduced, courage is amplified, and with courage comes the motivation, and will, to get out of our comfort zones and do sensational things!

This is when we feel ALIVE. And *Fabulous*!

With courage comes trying new things, and if we're not afraid of ,or attached to any result, then we can experience all manner of wonderful things—things we create or things that arise.

People often say that what holds them back from trying new things and *really* living life is a lack of confidence.

Hmmm. If I waited for confidence, I would never achieve a damn thing because it doesn't just show up!

Confidence comes from courage, and courage has been the key to my being able to do things I never thought were possible.

Courage is the key.
Courage is the key.
Courage is the key,

So give up trying to gain confidence.

Just focus on embracing everything about yourself and developing your courage so you can get out into the world and do things you'd like to do.

Fabulosity
is the HABIT of
embracing, **loving,** and ***trusting***
all aspects of YOURSELF
(good, bad, and ugly)
and
all aspects of your life
(past, present, and future)
so that ***fear is reduced,***
courage is ENHANCED
and you can
fully express yourself
to *live life* as an EXPERIMENT with
lightness,
curiosity,
and
a SENSE *of* ADVENTURE

Once fear is reduced and courage is enhanced, you will find it easier to step into the boldest version of yourself in all aspects, including how you express yourself.

In *Fabulosity*, "self-expression" is used in its broadest sense and has many facets. We'll unpack the facets that I think are critical to *Fabulosity*, starting with style, which is a topic I love and the facet that changed dramatically for me when I adopted *Fabulosity* as a life philosophy.

Expressing Yourself Through Style

Fully expressing who you are through your style is a true gift and one of the outcomes of living a *Fabulous* life. Dressing for yourself and wearing clothes that support who you want to be is bliss!

Style is often confused with fashion, but the difference is that style is about pleasing yourself, whereas fashion is about pleasing everyone else.

In my own life, I've leaned into my flamboyant tendencies and created a wardrobe of unusual clothes that I love. I've ditched all the rules and guidelines that supposedly make one "stylish," such as what colors to wear, what shapes flatter which body type, what makes someone look thinner, what should be worn to the office, what shouldn't be worn at a certain age, and, and, and.

My goal is no longer to look young, thin, or beautiful (more about this in the next section), which gives me enormous freedom in what I wear.

I've also removed anything that doesn't *feel* awesome or items that should work but just don't, for whatever reason. Anything that doesn't feel like 100% me-as-I-am-now has been moved on without guilt, shame, or explanation.

As a result, I have a more compact wardrobe consisting of clothes, shoes, accessories, and jewelry I love.

I don't worry about the past, what I used to wear, how my body looked, or, most of all, what other people might think! I wear the clothes that I want, whenever I want, and how I want, with the understanding that my style is evolving.

I find myself swapping between extremes.

Sometimes I like bold and bright, and other times I like black and minimalist.

Before *Fabulous* (BF), I thought I had to choose my "look" and stick to a certain style personality (as per many of the gurus out there). Now I know in my bones that I'm multi-faceted, and I can look different every day if I want to. I switch between bohemian, Gothic, steampunk-inspired, artsy, and white minimalist.

Sometimes I wear a lot of accessories; other times, I wear hardly any.

> *Fabulous self-expression is a delicious form of selfishness that's good for everyone—it makes you feel Fabulous, which in turn gives other people the inspiration to find their own Fabulous.*

Having said that, it can happen that when you dress for your own pleasure, you come across women (and men) who feel intimidated by your freedom of expression and energy.

If that happens to you, don't be deterred. Partners, friends, and family may need some time to adjust to the new you, and they might feel uncomfortable in the beginning.

Or they might never adjust to your new style.

Strangers might react in negative ways too.

I remember once going into a local community shop, wearing a denim jacket with an enormous flower brooch. The woman behind the counter quipped,

> "Why are you wearing that? To attract attention?"

This comment is a clear indication of someone who most definitely is not living in the *Fabosphere*!

If negative reactions happen to you, maintain your high vibration, react with love, and don't be attached to receiving acceptance or approval from anyone other than yourself.

You don't need it anymore!

We will talk more about style in Part IV when we dive into the FIFI Formula.

Rejecting Young, Thin, And Beautiful (YTB)

We cannot talk about style, or even *Fabulosity*, without discussing the elephant in the room: the dreaded expectation of today's women to look young, thin, and beautiful, or "YTB" for short. YTB sounds like a serious health condition, and that's exactly what it is!

Unfortunately, YTB is the scourge of modern society, and it's responsible for so much misery. In a nutshell, we are constantly shown and told that if we are not YTB, then we are lesser human beings.

> *It is often a major contributor to midlife women feeling invisible, irrelevant, and like their best days are behind them. This is simply not true!*

YTB is also the epitome of perfectionism, which is the antithesis of *Fabulosity*.

Perfectionism—and striving for it—is so goddamn boring, unnecessary, and life-sucking. It's time we eradicated it! For me, even looking at perfection is boring. Give me wrinkles, vintage, mismatched and character any day.

What's the *Fabulous* response to YTB? One response is to adopt the attitude of the ladies and gentlemen of the Advanced Style Movement, who will never be invisible or irrelevant, and whose best days are most certainly not behind them.

> They do not strive for YTB, perfectionism, or even being "age-appropriate." Instead, they embody *Fabulosity*—striving to look, feel, and do *Fabulous*, and without worrying about what society thinks.
> The funny thing is that when they show up in "full feather," they attract a lot of attention.

People LOVE seeing them live their daily lives in spectacular fashion (pardon the pun).

They are vital, energizing people who inspire others, even young people who admit to aspiring to be like them when they get older. Do they live a perfect life? Of course not. Everyone has an imperfect life with pain and suffering.

Every life stage has issues and challenges.

This somehow gets forgotten whenever people lament the physical and mental aches and pains that come with aging.

If I looked back on my life, I'd be able to find loads of things to complain about in every decade.

My teenage years were no walk in the park.

In my twenties, I felt all sorts of pressure to conform, get married, have children, find the right career, find the right relationship, and more.

My thirties were spent bearing children, retching from morning sickness, dealing with a changing body, having worries about what schools to choose, who would look after my kids if I died, earning money to buy a family home, and, and, and.

Every age and stage has its problems and beauty.

When you live in the *Fabosphere*, your self-expression is not based on YTB. Society is agist, sexist, lookist, and misogynistic; we need to take a stand by:

showing up in *Fabulous* energy,
taking up space, believing and
demonstrating our value, staying
vivacious (nice word) in mind, body,
and spirit, calling out discrimination,
and showing younger generations that
maturity is a virtue.

We need to be:

living with purpose and pleasure,

playing bigger, proudly displaying our
wrinkles and gray hair, dressing
in a way that shows off our personality,
taking part in society in a full, confident way,
sharing our experience,
and spreading positivity.

Full-bodied self-expression is made easier when you embrace all that is and judge it all to be *Fabulous*. This leads to reduced fear, empowering you to unleash your courage to shake awake and strut, expressing yourself at whatever age or stage you find yourself at.

Later on, I'll talk about my *Fabulous* and practical antidote to YTB so have no fear!

Choosing Your Purpose

I believe that choosing your purpose is an important aspect of self-expression because most of us never think about it, let alone choose it and live it.

When I started to lean into *Fabulosity*, I realized that I had a new purpose:

To help women play bigger and bolder in the spirit of Fabulosity.

This came out of a deep desire to do the same for myself. This figures because what do they say about teaching? You teach best what you have to learn. And I'm very happy with that!

By habitually identifying as *Fabulous*, which felt so right to do, I discovered that I could package this purpose up in a flamboyant, unique wrapping called *Fabulosity*, which is a complete and total expression of the current me.

However, this wasn't always my purpose. For the last 20 years, my purpose has been to be someone else: a mother, wife, student, and seeker.

In the future, my purpose might become something completely different, based on who I want to be next and what my priorities become.

> *In Fabulosity, we work with the possibility that we don't find our purpose; we have many at different times in our lives.*

And purposes are not found or inherent; we create them based on who we've become.

For years, I've searched for my life purpose and felt like I'd "failed" because I couldn't find it. Some people are certain about their life purpose and have always known it.

If that's you, amazing! That's not me, and now that I'm leaning into the idea that I choose my purpose, a whole new world of possibility and pleasure is opening to me!

I feel that, whatever my current purpose is, I can go along with it with courage and joy — enjoying the ride, and seeing where it spits me out.

My purpose is not permanent. It evolves, just like me. Just like you. What an adventure!

> *I want every woman to express themselves fully, whether it's within their current purpose or a new one they're creating.*

I'd love for them to feel the magic and exhilaration of looking deep inside themselves to see what they have to offer or what they'd like to explore next, both in their professional and personal lives.

Taking Action

Self-expression in *Fabulosity* also implies taking action, for whatever reason.

I have an artist friend who is incredibly talented. She was hankering after an expensive machine that would allow her to make prints. She loved creating her unique style of art in this way. She had the financial means, the support of her husband, and the ideas to use it, but she held back from buying it. She could not bring herself to invest in the machine, believing on some level that she wasn't able to justify it.

Fabulosity says pleasure is a good enough reason for any action. In fact, any reason is good enough for any action.

In so many cases, taking action and going for it is the most obvious and *Fabulous* thing to do.

Oftentimes, we hold ourselves back from pleasure, freedom, spontaneity, and adventure... for no real good reason except some silly story.

Fabulosity thrives when, to co-opt the Nike slogan, we
JUST DO IT.

What's the worst that can happen when you do "it" with lightness, curiosity and a sense of adventure?

What's the worst that can happen when you know that there is no success or failure?

What's the worst that can happen if you realize that life is an experiment, and the outcome of anything you attempt is *Fabulous*?

Taking action puts you in the game, and being in the game is much more rewarding and fun than sitting on the sidelines.

Buy a wetsuit and get in the sea.
Invite someone you've just met to tea.
Sign up for that art class you've always wanted to do.
Take the first step towards starting your new business.

And for all those procrastinators, overthinkers or course junkies out there, remember that "knowing and not doing" is the same as "not knowing."

Sitting on an idea or talent is not *Fabulous*.

Get whatever you have out into the sunshine, however imperfect, and
  enjoy
    every moment of this
      roller coaster
        life.

Fabulosity
is the HABIT of
embracing, **loving,** and ***trusting***
all aspects of YOURSELF
(good, bad, and ugly)
and
all aspects of your life
(past, present, and future)
so that ***fear is reduced,***
courage is ENHANCED
and you can
fully express yourself
to *live life* as an EXPERIMENT with
lightness,
curiosity,
and
a SENSE *of* ADVENTURE

This is probably my favorite line of the definition. I mean, if you're not convinced about *Fabulosity* yet, surely there is nothing more delicious than living life as an experiment, where no outcome is expected?

I propose that if people lived life as an experiment, they would not be scared of failure or success, because there is none. Whatever the outcome, there is no judgment, only learning and accomplishment that the experiment has been executed!

Surely we would live bolder, more passionately, and more courageously because we have absolutely nothing to lose and everything to gain by simply doing.

We would all be on a level playing field. We are all just scientists conducting our own life experiments and sharing the results with interested onlookers. There's no pressure to be anyone other than who you want to be, for no reason other than to see what it would be like. No pressure, just pleasure!

Ralph Waldo Emerson said,

"The journey is the destination."

I'd like to *Fabify* this to:

The journey is the EXPERIMENT and the destination.

Fabulosity
is the HABIT of
embracing, **loving,** and *trusting*
all aspects of YOURSELF
(good, bad, and ugly)
and
all aspects of your life
(past, present, and future)
so that *fear is reduced,*
courage is ENHANCED
and you can
fully express yourself
to *live life* as an EXPERIMENT with
lightness,
curiosity,
and
a SENSE *of* ADVENTURE

Lightening Up

Some people are naturally inclined to hop and skip through life, somehow managing to not take things too seriously. I was not born with that gene.

I was a serious child, and even as an adult I tend to take life too seriously if I don't check myself.

Fabulosity has been truly fantastic in helping me simply lighten up because, if you think about it, when you decide and believe everything that happens is *Fabulous*, then it's much easier to simply enjoy life, even in all its complexity.

If fear is reduced and courage enhanced, suddenly you feel like you can do things! And if you feel that life is an experiment, then a whole world of possibility opens up!

This allows you to energetically laugh and dance through the good times and even some of the not-so-good times. It's all good. It makes it a pleasure to experience everything that this mortal coil has to offer.

Being Curious

Curiosity is an often-overlooked virtue that features strongly in *Fabulosity*. It's what keeps us zestful, vibrant, interesting, and feeling alive.

> *It helps us stay motivated, engaged with life, and open to new experiences. It's the very lifeblood of creativity, happiness, and indeed, Fabulosity! Without it, there is no means to expand, discover, or thrive.*

To me, living with curiosity means being actively engrossed -and fully engaged- in everything that's going on in my life. I've created an insatiable appetite to learn about absolutely everything; the more obscure, the better.

I want to meet new people from different backgrounds, experiences, and viewpoints. I want to throw myself into projects, not raising my head to do anything else unless I have to. I want to try every food and visit every country. I want to savor the experience of everything new, novel, and compelling.

In the spirit of *Fabulosity*, I invite you to be intentional about your curiosity. It's an awesome feeling to be absorbed in everything around you.

> It's like being in the world's most bounteous candy store, where you are surrounded by the most incredible array of deliciousness you can imagine.

Everywhere you look, there are delights to tempt your every sense and taste bud.

Curiosity didn't kill the cat. It took the cat on an exciting excursion into the thrilling unknown!

Having A Sense Of Adventure

Oh, sense of adventure—how do I love thee? Let me count the ways.

We are on this mortal coil for the tiniest amount of time, so we must be sure not to squander the chance to explore every opportunity, every emotion, and every pleasure with an open-hearted sense of adventure.

Nothing in life is guaranteed, and no one is born with a road map or tutorial on how to navigate our time on Earth. What an awfully exciting, once-in-a-lifetime experience that surely must be embarked upon with feelings of titillation and anticipation!

No one is getting out alive, so we have the choice to either go for it, see what we can pull off, and get high on the experience, or we can simply mutter and moan, stagnate, and coast. *Fabulosity* is about going for it.

> Think of life as freewheeling down a hill
> on a bicycle:wind blowing through your hair,
> holding tight during the speed wobbles,
> dusting off after the falls,
> and getting straight back on,
> steering as best you can, but
> delighting in the idea that who
> knows where you will
> finally stop.

Having a sense of adventure is an element of the Fabulosity process that is incredibly under-expressed in modern society. But not anymore!

The Story So Far

That's it, and there you have it. This is the full, unabridged definition of *Fabulosity* and hopefully by now you're feeling it!

> *Fabulosity is a habit and a life philosophy, but it's also a spirit and an energy that cannot be contained.*

Once you've had a taste of it, you'll want more, and you'll want to liberally scatter it around.

Whenever I think of spreading *Fabulosity*, I always think of that gorgeous clip in the movie Mama Mia, where all the women throw off their bundles of wood and washing baskets, and they all skip and dance to the waterside.

Through the screen, you can just feel their sense of joy, freedom, and lightness as all these women decide to give in to the magic of life. Even if it's just for a few minutes in their daily routine.

Can you imagine if we tackled all our daily and life events with that level of *joie de vivre*?

> *Fabulosity is available to everyone, as long as they decide to choose it.*

For clarity's sake, I'd now like to go into what it's not.

YOUR LIFE IS AN EXPERIMENT

What Fabulosity Isn't

It's Not About Being Extroverted, Unless It Is

You might think that *Fabulosity* is an ostentatious concept that will suit only extroverts, but I invite you to consider that it's the opposite— completely subjective, and therefore available to all energies.

It is the fullest expression of you, even if that expression is quiet and reserved, serious, and deep. The world desperately needs its introverts to look, feel, and do *Fabulous* in their own way so they can come out and play. We need them to show up boldly and bring their wisdom and insights out into the open where they can make a difference.

On the other hand, if you are an extrovert, then *Fabulosity* invites you to shine your brightest light.

> *Be the boldest, brightest version of yourself, and seek out people who will appreciate you.*

If you are the sun, be the sun. If you are the moon, be the moon. We need both to shine.

It's Not About Perfection

Fabulosity is not about creating a perfect life filled with love hearts, palm trees, and unicorns. How boring!

Forget the perfect body, perfect relationship, perfect house, perfect children, perfect moment, and the perfect style. The fabulisciousness is in the imperfection, the flaws, the character, the learning, the warts, and the uniqueness of everything that is you.

Give up the ideal of perfection. Perfection is a story that keeps us stuck. Start where you are, today. Get into the game, whatever that is, and start to experiment.

It's Not Frivolous Or Childish

Fabulosity is not frivolous. If you look below the surface, it is complex, multi-layered, and deep.

It's about digging into the depths of your soul with courage and activation to find the diamond that is you and then liberating it without apology or filter, but instead with glee and spirit.

It's about showing up, even if you're scared—or because you're scared—and showing the world who you are and who you want to be.

This is extremely powerful!

Letting out the most *Fabulous* version of yourself is not frivolous.

It's power.

It's Not About Flamboyance, Unless It Is

So many of us have been told our whole lives to "quiet down." Don't make waves. Don't shine too bright. Don't be too loud.

As women, our visibility, mixed with our innate gifts and wisdom, has gotten us killed, burned, raped, and damaged by those who are unable to handle it.

In modern-day society, we are constantly told that we are too old, too thin, too fat, too wrinkled, too bold, too poor, too rich, too much, too colorful, not colorful enough, too outspoken, too meek—the list goes on.

We are constantly told we can't, must, should, or shouldn't. We must wear these colors because they make us look good. Don't wear this because it makes you look old. Don't. Do. Don't. Do.

Fabulosity says if you are flamboyant, or want to be, let it out. And if flamboyance is not your style, do *Fabulous* your way.

> *You don't have to be flamboyant to be Fabulous, but if you want to, you can!*

Fabulosity says to do, say, wear, think, and feel what makes you come alive. There will be people who love it, and those who don't. You are not here to please anyone.

It's Not Toxic Positivity

Toxic positivity is when you invalidate feelings by putting a positive spin on everything. *Fabulosity* is not that.

It's about understanding that everything that happens to us, whether you judge it to be good or bad, is part of life's rich tapestry.

That makes it *Fabulous* and should be embraced, loved, and trusted as an essential part of our journey.

When times are tough, there is no sense in pretending that you're having fun.

During those times, get the support you need from family, friends, and professionals until change takes place and those times pass.

Learn the lessons these tricky times surely have for you and be grateful for them, for they are the building blocks of who you are.

Is there any other way to look at life that's more *Fabulous*?

It's Not About Excess Or Materialism

Fabulosity is a flamboyant concept and could be interpreted as promoting overconsumption, arrogance, bombast, a lack of moderation, or even waste. It's not.

The only excess that *Fabulosity* concerns itself with is expansiveness, generosity of spirit and action, and creating MORE of the stuff that makes life worthwhile and meaningful, like positivity, hope, love, aliveness, possibility, and pleasure.

Fabulosity is not about materialism, but that's not to say you can't enjoy material things.

> *If you want to surround yourself with curated, much-loved, beautiful, quality things that bring you joy, that's a Fabulous thing to do.*

Enjoy them and share them with people that matter to you.

It's Not Reserved For The Good Times

Fabulosity is for everyone at any time, and it's yours to harness whenever you want it, no matter your circumstances.

> *If you're going through a tough time and feel anything but Fabulous, that's exactly when you can start the Fabification process.*

Start small. It gets easier as it becomes a habit.

If you're struggling financially, you are more likely to attract and be open to more opportunities and money if you live in the spirit of *Fabulosity* than if you don't.

At minimum, you will feel differently about your struggle.

Similarly, if you've got health issues, *Fabulosity* will help you count your blessings and create more of a foundation for healing than otherwise.

The same applies to relationships—in fact, I can't think of any situation where it doesn't apply in some shape or form.

It's Not About Extreme Go-Getting

Living in the *Fabosphere* is not about pushing yourself to the max, striving for impossible standards, or putting pressure on yourself to constantly improve. Being *Fabulous* doesn't mean you're on a non-stop hustle to be better.

Instead, we recognize that a life well lived is characterized by creating moments of tranquility when we feel like it, exploring new frontiers inside and outside of ourselves with no attachment to outcomes, and having appreciation for the present, amongst other thing.

We exist as humans to savor life's simple pleasures - all of them.

The Story So Far

Are you still with me? How are you doing?

We've delved into what *Fabulosity* is and isn't.

Next, I'm going into the foundations of *Fabulosity*—there are only three of them, and I lovingly call them the Three Permissions.

FABULOSITY
IS
FREEDOM

The Three Permissions

Fabulosity* has three delicious tenets, or pillars, that I call "Permissions". They seem innocuous, but are in fact so energizing that they alone will improve your life if you apply them.

Why do I call them Permissions? Well, for some reason, it seems that permission is what many women need. We're often not great at doing things for no reason at all other than because we want to. Or because it's fun. Or because we can.

Even if we have "legitimate" reasons, we somehow need to justify them to ourselves or others.

I know this for myself. Even as the self-proclaimed Queen of *Fabulosity*, I need to work hard to allow myself to do certain things without justification or guilt. The "Permissions" give me the energetic go-ahead to be *Fabulous* in whatever shape or form, whenever I want to!

What are the Permissions?

Celebration, Reinvention and Fabification.

Let's explore them a little more, starting with Celebration.

CELEBRATION

The ability to celebrate life with all it entails seems to be diminishing in modern life.

We are so busy juggling activities that we don't pause nearly enough to celebrate what we have or where we are. This is a great shame because celebration is important for so many reasons:

Marking important events

Celebrations are important for acknowledging and commemorating life's greatest achievements and milestones, including birthdays, weddings, graduations, promotions, and other significant life events. They give us the opportunity to reflect on what these mean to us and acknowledge the work and journey it took to get us here.

Building connections

Celebrations bring people together, helping to strengthen and build relationships. Celebrating with all the people that matter to us—friends and family, our community, and our work colleagues—allows us to connect on a deeper level and build shared experiences and memories.

Boosting morale

Celebrations can provide much-needed boosts to morale and motivation, both in personal and professional settings. By taking the time to acknowledge and celebrate accomplishments, we can feel more confident, motivated, and inspired to achieve more.

Providing closure
Celebrations can also provide a sense of closure, particularly for events that have been life-altering or difficult. By celebrating the end of difficult periods, it helps us to see the lessons and perhaps even the blessings of them, so that we can move on with our life experiment.

The "*Fabulous* life" incorporates various intensities and scales of celebration every day. Let's explore some ideas, starting with the low-key end of the scale: Gratitude.

Gratitude

Practicing gratitude has many mind-body-spirit benefits.

Gratitude strengthens relationships, increases positive emotions, and reduces negative ones. It also helps shift focus from worries to positive thoughts, reducing stress during the day and improving sleep quality and duration at night.

Practicing gratitude builds resilience, enabling us to better cope with adversity and leading to health benefits such as improved immune function and lower levels of inflammation.

Gratitude is most definitely a habit and something to intentionally practice as often as possible every day. Unless you specifically want to, you don't need to make any special time to do it.

> *Just do it in whichever way feels good for you, and make it as long as you want.*

At the very least, start every morning with thoughts about things you're grateful for, even if it's just three things.

I've recently discovered the joys of gratitude journals, which are usually beautifully illustrated bundles of joy, providing awesome little prompts and affirmations for daily gratitude practice.

They're a great way to build the habit of self-love and gratitude, and I adore them so much that I've started designing and publishing my own!

During times of life that are particularly testing, you might find it difficult to summon up feelings of gratitude. I go through the motions anyway, letting the automation of the habit sweep me along. Even if I'm not "feeling" it particularly, just saying the words often puts me in a better frame of mind. I don't always succeed, but that's fine.

Nothing in life is perfect, I remind myself.
I just do the best I can in the spirit of lightness.

Rituals

Family and personal rituals are a totally underrated yet rewarding way to celebrate being alive, and, in the *Fabosphere*, we try to create them wherever possible. Let's explore a little about why they benefit us as humans:

Rituals create a sense of order and structure

By performing familiar rituals, we can establish a sense of routine that gives groups of people like families, friendship groups, work colleagues, and communities predictability and structure, which is comforting, especially in times of change or uncertainty.

Rituals foster a sense of community and belonging

By participating in rituals together with others, we can feel a deep connection and fellowship, which builds our self-esteem, gives us a sense of belonging, and reduces loneliness and anxiety.

Rituals provide comfort and healing in times of grief or loss

They can help us process our emotions and find closure. They can help us feel like we're part of a greater whole—something bigger than ourselves.

Rituals cultivate mindfulness and presence in our daily lives

By performing any action with intention, which is what rituals are, we can cultivate a sense of mindfulness and awareness, allowing for feelings of gratitude, pleasure, and joy.

There are so many good reasons to have rituals, but what I love about them is that they're not only fun to create and experience but also bring us joy in the delightful anticipation of them.

I'll never forget when my eldest son left home for the first time for university in the Netherlands. He was never a particularly sentimental type of person, but suddenly he was so excited about our plans for that year's Christmas—not for the presents, but for the very specific rituals that we've been practicing in our family for the last decade.

In our family, Christmas is celebrated at my in-laws, starting on December 23rd. On Christmas Eve, we spend the day decorating the tree and setting the table for our Christmas meal, which we have that same evening rather than on Christmas day. Before bed, we sprinkle some home-made reindeer food (oats mixed with glitter) on the driveway and lay out mince pies and whiskey for Father Christmas (which he really appreciates!).

On Christmas Day, the young wake up to find their bedside Christmas stockings filled with little gifts, including the traditional orange. Around 9 a.m, everyone is usually up and about, and with cups of coffee in hand, we sit down to the ritual of opening presents one by one.

The young take turns handing out the gifts, which have all been beautifully wrapped in newspaper and decorated with drawings and second-hand trinkets (a tradition we started for environmental reasons).

At around 10 a.m., we go off to the local church for the Christmas service.
Christmas Day dinner is leftovers, followed by a few games of Canasta (a card game). On Boxing Day, we go for a family walk in the countryside, relax by the fire, and then attend a pantomime play at the local theater.

It's a ritual that's evolved over the years and no doubt will continue to evolve as the children grow up and circumstances change, but these rituals create memories that last forever.

Another example from our own family is that we celebrate birthdays over three days, an idea we borrowed from a dear friend of mine.
The three days have names: Birthday Eve (borrowed from Christmas Eve), Birth Day, and Boxing Birth Day (the day after Birth Day).
The person celebrating their birthday gets to choose the meals on those days and is generally spoiled.
Present-opening is a group ritual in itself, held on our bed on Birth Day morning, with all family members tuning in via Zoom if they're not physically present.
When our youngest son was around five years old, his opportunistic tendencies came to the fore when he suggested that we extend birthday celebrations even further.
He thought we might create Birthday Adam (because Adam came before Eve) and Bruise Day (which comes after Boxing Birth Day and when you're full of bruises from being boxed!). We still laugh about this to this day.
Rituals are easily incorporated into our lives if we're a little bit intentional about them.

Some examples are lighting candles at dinner time, having family games night on Fridays, and saying "I love you" as the last thing you say to someone every evening.
All families have some rituals, particularly around milestone events, but I believe that with a little bit of

imagination and intention, we can and should create more rituals in our daily routines as opportunities to create richer lives.

Enjoy Everything

An elderly friend of mine introduced me to the concept of "Enjoy Everything." She uses it at every opportunity, especially when she says goodbye to friends after visiting. I've adopted this ritual too, and I love it.

Having the intention to enjoy everything immediately puts you not only in a positive frame of mind but also in the present. It makes you conscious of savoring every moment, no matter how mundane or insignificant, because every moment that we live intentionally is another reminder that we are ALIVE.

"Enjoy everything" is a command from your head to your heart, a mini celebration that is simple to do. As a mantra, it can be quite life-changing.

Creative Projects

It's human nature to want to create beautiful things, and we've been doing so since the year dot. But being creative is not on the radar for most people, and it's certainly not usually thought of as a way to celebrate life.

I guess there are so many things that vie for our attention every day that perhaps we simply lack the energy to prioritize creative projects.

Or maybe creativity was never a "thing" growing up, or we just don't believe that we are creative.

Or perhaps we are so stuck in perfectionism or the fear of failure that we don't believe we are capable of creating anything worthwhile, so we don't try.

Whatever the reasons keeping you from being creative, I invite you to create a new story and introduce this form of celebration into your life as often as possible.

Creativity comes in many forms and depends on your personality, energy levels, and circumstances. It includes, but is not limited to:
events, art, cooking, interior decorating, sewing, poetry, gardening, singing, baking, basket weaving, coloring, rearranging furniture in your home, decluttering, and playing a musical instrument,

...any projects where you change, improve, or create something that wasn't there before, preferably something "beautiful".

Of course, we know that beauty is in the eye of the beholder, and perfection doesn't exist, so don't compare your output to anyone else's.

The point is to celebrate being alive by creating something that attempts to improve your world in some way.

If your project doesn't work out, it doesn't matter. Do it for fun, or try to improve it. Or simply start another.

Create from where you are; start now, start small, and enjoy the journey.

Pain And Suffering Rewards

This form of celebration is big in our family, and it's helped us to celebrate the more unpleasant of life's experiences (let's call them "nasties"- the plural of "nasty") by distracting us and giving us something *Fabulous* to focus on.

It's an amusing name that immediately makes you smile, even before implementation!

The idea is to reward yourself for nasties— anything from a scary dentist appointment or an upsetting breakup to a difficult conversation you need to have with someone or a completed challenge.

If you know upfront what your Pain And Suffering Reward will be, you'll have something to look forward to. Pre-planned Rewards are the most popular in our family because you can talk about them as a way to offset the emotions and thoughts around the nasty in question.

Rewards can also be spontaneous and on-thespot if the spirit or an upcoming nasty occasion calls for them. There are no rules about when they are appropriate or not!

A Reward could be anything big or small, tangible or experiential.
Some examples are: a weekend away, a day off, chocolate, an item of jewelry you've had your eye on, a new outfit, a book, a facial, or a massage—whatever lights you up.

Jollification

I love this word! Jollification is the party side of the Celebration Permission and is defined as "a lively celebration with others; merrymaking."

The most obvious jollification opportunity, which many people fail to do anything about, is birthdays. Yes, people might celebrate big birthdays, but most birthdays come and go without ceremony.
Why?
Here's the truth: It's always worth celebrating another successful trip around the sun because if you took the time to really think about all the things you've survived to do so, you would be dancing naked on the ceiling fan and shouting the *hallelujah* chorus!
Many people do not make it to their next birthday, and it's easy to take life and everything in it for granted.
Do not take your life, your loved ones, or your birthday for granted.
Celebrate every year, including everything you've experienced (good and so-called "bad") that year.
Does it need to be full-scale jollification? No, but give yourself permission to mark the occasion in any shape or form. And when the big birthdays come around, definitely celebrate those in a special way! Fill up your heart like a balloon—fill it with love, light, and fire.
When your birthday is over, you can look to other days to jollify. You can even make them up as you go along because there are no rules with *Fabulosity*!

Mondays are good days for jollification. So are first-time anythings. Or last-time anythings. Any milestone, achievement, or non-achievement.

Find any excuse to celebrate through jollification, in any way you can dream up.

Use your best china for your celebrations. Dress up in *Fabulous* clothes—ones that you keep at the back of your closet. Employ all your fancy tablecloths, glasses, and knickknacks. Crack open the champagne for no reason at all. Invite friends around. Family. Your neighbor. Any excuse for a party!

Please allow yourself to celebrate living, in any shape or form, often. All these things add up to lighting up your life.

So, those are just some ideas for the Celebration Permission. Let's move on to the next Permission: Reinvention. Another goodie!

REINVENTION

The second of the Three Permissions is Reinvention, which I also like to call "Active Reinvention."

In my definition, this is something along the lines of

"the spectacular act of intentionally and deliciously upgrading—or transforming—yourself or your circumstance into a more expansive, fresher, or remarkably different version."

Savvy celebrities reinvent all the time because they know it's necessary to stay relevant and inspirational to their fans.

Active Reinvention is something that's available to all of us at any age in many ways, and it gives us the opportunity to explore the dormant or unknown faces of our abounding, multi-faceted selves.

We CAN become someone new at *anytime* in our careers, relationships, hobbies, worldview, self-identity, personal brand, sexual orientation, style, and every other aspect of our lives.

And, if we allow ourselves, we CAN do new, unpredictable, and different things.

As an example from my own life, I've undergone various reinventions. Like when I decided to give up my career in public relations to become a *Fabulous* Coach.

This required a new identity, new skills, and courage!

Where I used to be more of a behind-the-scenes person, I've reinvented myself to be more in the public domain as an amateur actress, content producer, podcast host, and author. This was not expanding my comfort zone; it was shattering it, I can tell you! There was a lot of resistance along the way and a fair bit of tears and trauma trying to figure things out, feeling inadequate, and questioning myself often. Like we all do when we decide to make a change.

I'm still constantly reinventing myself wherever I can, including my style and hair, and I'm always on the lookout to discover new ways of thinking and living.

Although reinvention is something we can all do, many of us avoid it because change can be painful, as we all know.

It means getting out of familiar territory and launching into the unknown, which can be very scary.

We may also face opposition from other people, particularly the people who are closest to us. The last thing we want to hear is:

You're not the same person I met.
I don't recognize you anymore.
You've changed.
Who do you think you are?

I know I've been faced with these allegations, but I've decided to count them as compliments because I would like my life to be filled with many iterations of me!

I want to see the world through the eyes of many different "me"s.

I want to grow and change. I find this quest absolutely delightful (most days, not all), and it keeps my spirit and energy youthful and vital.

Authenticity

In my experience, one of the obstacles to Active Reinvention is something that is not often thought of or spoken of as an "obstacle." It's *authenticity*. I touched on it earlier in the section on You 2.0, but I'd like to explore it a little more in the context of Active Reinvention.

On the surface, authenticity is a positive, aspirational trait, especially if, for example, you are living inauthentically as a people-pleaser. People-pleasing is a disempowering habit that often occurs at the expense of one's own happiness and truth.

However, I think authenticity can often be confused with "familiarity," and this is where I think the problem comes in.

Authenticity and familiarity give us the same wonderful, oozy feelings of warmth and security, but they are different things.

If the two are categorized as the same thing, we can get stuck in our comfort zone, the place where nothing exciting or invigorating ever occurs.

Staying in your familiar zone inhibits personal growth, reinvention, and often prevents us from embarking on character-building escapades.

To illustrate, you might say you can't do solo travel because you're a homebody. Therefore, being a homebody is authentic to you.

Could it be that being a homebody feels authentic to you only because it's familiar? Maybe solo travel feels "inauthentic" to you only because it's uncomfortable and unfamiliar.

This is a *comfort zone* issue, not an authenticity issue.

What if you decide to test your own boundaries and embark on a solo trip, lets say to Barbados, and then discover that you really love traveling alone? Solo travel thus becomes part of who you are. It was always there, it was just hidden because it was an unexplored, unknown part of you.

We are multi-faceted, with many facets remaining hidden until we discover them (by leaving our comfort zone).

Plus, we also change over time, which means something that wasn't authentic to us in the past can most definitely become authentic to us in the future.

In my opinion, authenticity isn't always what it seems, and the search for it can inhibit self-development and e x h i l a r a t i o n
if we confuse it with familiarity.

Changing And Evolving

Fabulosity gives us permission to change and evolve.

Yes, I know that this is a strange sentence because we're adults and we don't need permission to do anything. Except that I see evidence to the contrary on a daily basis. Here are two examples from my own life of how this can play out:

My daughter's friend knew from a young age that when she left school she was going to study nursing. But when the time finally came to pack up her school books for the last time, she had the urge to go off to Italy to work as an *au pair*. Out of the blue, she wanted to experience a different way of life before settling down to her studies.

She was so full of anguish about this change of heart, feeling like she was "selfish" because she was following her bliss. Luckily, she dug deep for her courage, gave herself permission to be young and free, and, at the last minute, went off to Rome. She's still there six months later and having a wonderful time!

Isn't that awesome?

By contrast, a young guy I heard about studied accounting at college but quickly realized he didn't like it. But, he didn't want to appear flaky, so he ignored what his heart was telling him, finished his studies and looked for an accounting job, where he spent his days feeling unfulfilled and uninspired. This young chap needs to learn to give himself permission to change his mind, live his life and find his bliss, no matter how it appears.

Fabulosity gives you the freedom, and invitation, to reinvent yourself, and to do it often, either in spectacular or micro ways.

Remember, the *Fabulous* life is about loving everything about yourself and your life so that you can fully express yourself in whichever ways you want to! That leaves plenty of scope for Active Reinvention whenever you feel like it, in whichever way feels good! There is no success or failure, only experimentation, adventure, and *Fabulosity!*

Opportunities For Active Reinvention

Mother Nature gives us many opportunities to create new beginnings, as painful or joyful as they might be.

The more character-building events might include big birthdays, divorce or separation, job loss, and illness.

As I mentioned earlier, don't waste a good crisis. I say feel the pain, learn the lessons quickly, and then reinvent!

The more joyful reinvention opportunities might include a new job, a new relationship, giving up smoking, moving to a new home, or buying a new car. I'll mention big birthdays again because they should be viewed in a positive light and should definitely be used as an opportunity to regenerate, revitalize, and reinvigorate—choose your "re"!

Or we can make liberal use of "excuses" for reinvention, like Mondays, every morning, Dry January, Lent, International Women's Day, and more.

Be imaginative!

Reinvent your identity, or parts of it.
Reinvent your life—or parts of it—like your career, hobbies, wardrobe, or relationships.

So you fancy reinventing as a hairdresser? It could be in your spare time to start, if that works, but do as hairdressers do and "do" hair. Sign up for a hairdressing course or become an apprentice on the weekends. Practice on your kids!

Want to reinvent as an artist? Artists create. Go on, create. No one needs to see your art. Just do as artists do and see how it evolves.

What does Active Reinvention look like to you?
What aspect of yourself do you want to explore?

You decide which aspect, and you can make up the aspect if you need to. Remember, everything is a story. Choose your story about what's possible.

Give yourself permission to reinvent.

At the end of the day, reinvention makes you FEEL ALIVE. It takes you out of your comfort zone—the place where dreams go to die. The comfort zone makes us old, lazy, and boring which is the opposite of *Fabulous*.

FABIFICATION

The third of the Three Permissions is *Fabification*, the process of taking something bland, tired, or ordinary and improving it, either in dramatic fashion or through a series of small improvements or habits, all in the spirit of making it *Fabulous*.

The concept of improving your life through incremental improvements (micro habits) is not an original idea, but, with the "*Fabulous*" spin on it, it has a magical, contagious energy that, as mentioned earlier in the book, I used to effectively overcome my low mood, a.k.a. depression.

Fabification is now a "thing" and forms one of the pillars of the life philosophy of Fabulosity.

In my life, *Fabification* is an everyday word and goal for me now, and every time something is *Fabified*—no matter how small—I feel so delightfully and secretly pleased with myself, like I've got a superpower that no one else has.

My latest *Fabification* is the daily use of a new type of enamel-growing toothpaste powder. I'm so intrigued to see if tooth enamel grows back...

I'm also *Fabifying* my eyelashes by trying to grow them naturally with eyelash growth serum, and I'm trying to *Fabify* my nighttime routine by reading before lights out rather than scrolling reels.

These are silly examples, but the point is that *Fabification* is such an easy way to improve life.

It's fun and doable, even during difficult times.

It brings you into the present and helps raise your vibration, making you available to attract good, positive, incredible things into your life.

Decluttering

No discussion on Fabification can be complete without bringing up the subject of decluttering.

The two are mutually exclusive. Fabification—and Active Reinvention for that matter—simply cannot happen if you are living among the vestiges of the past.

The other day, I conducted a fascinating activity with my family. I asked them to list which of their most beloved possessions (excluding humans, pets, and photographs) they would save if our home went up in flames.

The answers were surprising.

All of us named fewer than seven items. Seven!

Yet our house is filled with hundreds of items that we mistakenly believe we need, want, or love.

With this realization, we've been embarking on regular decluttering sessions where we ruthlessly donate and throw out items that simply do not serve the people we want to be.

There is always work to be done on this front, but over the last decade we have probably halved our possessions, including our book collection. Every time I declutter the house, I feel a physical sense of relief, spaciousness, and freedom. I can think much more clearly, and there's an inexplicable sense of calm and order in the house.

A friend of mine, who is a professional organizer, reminded me that when you get rid of the old, you make space for the new. And that's what Fabulosity is all about!

Avoidable Regrets

Have you ever come across a study on the elderly and what they would do differently if they had their time over again?

I've seen a few. They're fascinating and are good reminders to make the most of every moment we have on this planet.

I believe the Three Permissions go a long way in preventing some of the regrets that old people express. Let's explore some of their regrets:

> Not following their dreams or passions but instead pursuing a career or life path that they didn't truly enjoy.
>
> Not spending enough time with loved ones, family, or friends.
>
> Not expressing their true feelings or opinions to those around them.
>
> Not taking better care of their physical and mental health, such as exercising or seeking treatment for mental illness.
>
> Not traveling or experiencing new cultures.
>
> Not pursuing an education or learning new skills.

> Not saving or investing money earlier in life.
>
> Not taking enough risks or trying new things.
>
> Not being more assertive and standing up for themselves or their beliefs.
>
> Not living in the moment or appreciating the present, instead worrying about the past or future.

Did you notice that all the regrets are about things they didn't do, not what they did!

One of the most powerful things a life coach friend of mine said was that death sits on your right shoulder.

He made me look at my right shoulder to emphasize his point. We think we have time, but we just never know when our time will be up. We cannot waste any more of it living in a state that is anything other than *Fabulous*!

The Story So Far

I read somewhere that one of the big differences between the sexes is that women "ask permission," whereas men "proceed until apprehended."

I don't want to ask permission anymore. I hereby give myself the Three Permissions to Celebrate, Reinvent, and *Fabify* the hell out of anything and everything I choose. I invite you to do the same!

Let's move on now to Part IV, where I want to explore my antidote to our unrealistic expectations that we look Young, Thin, and Beautiful (YTB) forever.

Fabulosity is the most unselfish form of selfishness.

Yolanda Drewell

PART IV

WELCOME TO THAT FABULOUS FEELING!

The Fabuli Archetype

I love the concept of archetypes. I like to think of them as personality markers that provide a magical way for us to understand ourselves and our place in the world.

Archetypes are found in mythology, literature, and popular culture, and they're really useful in helping with our self-identity.

There are quite a few feminine archetypes, all of which have good sides and shadow sides (all *Fabulous*, remember), and I think they're great jumping-off points to explore You 2.0.

Some popular feminine archetypes include Mother, Maiden, Huntress, Mystic, and Lover. I like the sound of all of these, but the archetypes I'm most interested in for the purposes of *Fabulosity* are those for midlife and postmenopausal women.

Much to my chagrin, it appears that the most common archetype for the mature woman is the Wise Woman, a.k.a. the Crone.

CRONE?
Are you kidding me?

What is the picture that comes to mind when you think of a Crone? For me, it's some kind of really old, hideous, bent-over crazy woman or witch, or some version of that.

That's not the picture of aging that I have in my mind!
Is it yours?

Whether or not you resonate with the Crone, I decided that *Fabulosity* calls for its very own archetype, one with a much more compelling and juicier name.

I've called her Fabuli.

> *The Fabuli archetype is the embodiment of everything universally Fabulous.*
>
> *She is a lively modern woman, growing every day in confidence, activation, and courage, expanding into unexplored facets of herself, taking life with a pinch of salt, creating pleasure, and enjoying everything.*

Next are some examples of how the Fabuli might aspire to feel, do, and think.

THE
TRAITS
OF THE
FABULI

FEEL

Grateful

She feels thankful for all the good in her life,
and she is able to appreciate the people
and experiences that help her lead a rich, full life.

Confident

She feels confident in her abilities and decisions,
trusting that she can successfully navigate challenges
for her own good.

Empowered

She feels empowered to take control of her life
and make choices aligned with her
You 2.0 values and goals.

Inspired

She feels inspired by the people and experiences
around her and is motivated to pursue her passions
and life on her own terms where possible.

Activated

She feels activated, energized, and enthusiastic
about her daily life, pursuing new challenges
and opportunities for learning.

Peaceful

She feels a sense of inner peace,
despite her challenges.

Connected

She feels connected to the people in her life,
and certain of her place in her family,
friendship circles, community, and society.

Joyful

She feels joyful and happy most of the time, finding
pleasure in simple things and big moments.

Optimistic

She feels positive and optimistic about the future
and its possibilities.

Fulfilled

She feels fulfilled by the meaningful relationships,
experiences, and accomplishments in her life.

DO

Explores

The Fabuli takes advantage of opportunities to explore new places and cultures through books, meet-ups, seminars, and also real travel, both locally and internationally.

Learns

She loves to learn new things, and is always busy with ongoing learning, whether through formal education or simply seeking out new experiences and knowledge through books, meeting new people, courses, and whatever other opportunities come her way.

Connects with others

She leans into building relationships with people from all walks of life, genuinely interested in their points of view and seeking deeper connections.

Explores hobbies and passions

The Fabuli enjoys hobbies, projects, and passions for the purpose of joy and fulfillment, or in some cases, mastery. These could include learning an instrument, playing a sport, or pursuing creative endeavors.

Practices mindfulness

The Fabuli regularly takes time for gratitude, self-love and reflection, cultivating a sense of inner peace, clarity, and joy.

Takes care of her health

She does her best to prioritize physical and
mental health by practicing self care, eating healthily,
and exercising in fun ways.

Gives back to her community

She does her bit for the community, whether through
volunteering, buying local, or contributing
to charitable causes wherever she can. And she loves it!

Knows what she wants

She knows what she wants, and sets
into motion thoughts and actions
to make them a reality.

Celebrates accomplishments

She loves to see how far she has come and takes
the time to appreciate and celebrate accomplishments,
no matter how big or small.

Embraces change and takes risks

She accepts that change is inevitable and desirable
and that new experiences keep her vital and active.

THINK

I am grateful for the blessings in my life.

I am capable of achieving my goals and dreams.

I am open to new experiences and
opportunities for growth.

I am worthy of love and respect.

I am proud of what I accomplish,
no matter how small.

I am willing to try new things and take risks.

I am responsible for my own
well-being and happiness.

I am connected to something
greater than myself.

I am committed to creating and living
a purposeful and fulfilling life.

I choose to focus on positivity.

This can all sound like a tall order. Does the Fabuli get it right all the time? Of course not. But as she consistently works on the habit of *Fabulosity*, in an imperfect way, she gets to spend more time at her highest vibration: thinking, feeling, and behaving in the most expansive way possible.

And when the tough times come, the Fabuli doesn't put on a brave face. She doesn't cover up emotional pain with false positivity. She acknowledges the challenges, seeks support, and works through them, knowing that everything is a growth experience for her highest good.

The Story So Far

We've covered how and what the Fabuli might feel, do, and think.

But what about how she looks?

When it comes to physical appearance and self image, the Fabuli is pragmatic, confident, and free.

Her self-expression in her clothes is based on one idea:

My body is the least interesting thing about me.

For the Fabuli, the condition of Young, Thin, and Beautiful (YTB) is not an issue, firstly because she thinks, feels, and ages *Fabulous* which has nothing to do with YTB.

And secondly, she has another secret weapon—the ultimate antidote called the FIFI Formula!

THE FIFI FORMULA

The FIFI Formula

"You're not pretty, and you'll never be pretty. But it doesn't matter. You have something much better: you have style."

This quote comes from the inimitable Iris Apfel (centenarian inspirationalist and maximalist) and is what someone told her when she was young.

I'm itching to Fabify it by upgrading the last part to: "...you have something much better: you have Fabulosity!"

Iris Apfel oozes Fabulosity, and she's also a great example of the FIFI Formula in action (unbeknownst to her).

For background, I think the FIFI Formula was already starting to form in my subconscious mind in my teens. I realized then already that youthful good looks don't last forever and I needed to develop other aspects of myself if I wanted long term progress, and a positive self-image in the aging process.

I was influenced by my mother, who taught me early on to never trade on your looks because when they fade, you'll have nothing to fall back on. This advice really stuck with me.

I was also influenced by an article that I read in my teens about businesswoman and celebrity, Barbara Corcoran. She told the story of when she worked in a restaurant in her youth and how one of the other waitresses, a buxom bombshell, was attracting all the attention and earning all the tips.

Her mom's advice to her was to make the most of her own attributes and to wear pigtails with ribbons. This worked really well, proving that we all have different assets and should use them to our advantage.

I'm not supporting the objectification of women, but I remember this excerpt so well from years ago because it made me realize that no matter what you judge yourself as lacking, there's always a way to make up for it with attributes that you do have.

The same is true for when we age.

There's always a way to get attention, be heard, and be seen, no matter the competition or circumstance.

I know a lot of women need to hear this because so many of us feel invisible and irrelevant when we reach a certain age.

I want age to be just a number, and although I can see the ravages of time on my face and body, like all of us, I

know that I don't need YTB to be happy, *Fabulous* or valuable to society.
I know I'll never be invisible, irrelevant, or feel like the best years are behind me. Wrinkles and an imperfect body have nothing to do with the impact I can make in the world, and they don't limit my experience of the world, or my happiness, in any way.
Why? Because I've decided to focus on the positive, adopt *Fabulosity* as a life philosophy, and deploy my secret weapon, FIFI!
But what exactly is FIFI?

FIFI is an acronym for *Fresh, Interesting, Fabulous,* and *Interested.*
This little formula is the antidote to dieting, fashion rules, and cosmetic surgery.
It's the answer to the impossible goal of looking YTB.
With FIFI, you get to be the most fascinating woman in any room, at any age or stage, outshining your younger, thinner, more "attractive", "successful," and "intelligent" counterparts in energy, vitality, charisma, and memorability.
Let's dive in.

FRESH

Fresh is the first "F" in the FIFI Formula and the antidote to *young*.

We all know that it's guaranteed that anyone trying to look young forever will fail. Yet, the nasty anti-aging industry is worth multiple billions of dollars and growing.
How is it that worldly, successful, and intelligent women (and men) fall victim to the idea that we can and should look young for as long as possible so that we can be seen as valuable members of society?
And it's not young people that are perpetuating this—it's the oldsters! The mature, senior captains of society—editors, CEOs, opinion leaders, and founders of big corporations. For sure, there are younger people among them, but on the whole, it's veterans who are the biggest perpetrators of sexism, ageism, sizeism, and lookism.

And, even worse, it's not just men but also women who use "isms" against their sisters!

Women are often the biggest critics of other women.

Women in power, but also ordinary women like you and me, are either active or passive perpetrators. How unfabulous is that?

How do we change it?

The most important action in any challenge is to unleash You 2.0 and the Fabuli archetype. This will help us step into our power and bypass societal beliefs. If we don't fall for the stories that we are too old or too young, too fat or too thin, or whatever, then we cannot perpetrate these stories.

> *We simply have to start by truly believing we are Fabulous at any age and stage, and behave in a more empowered way.*

When we ourselves look, feel, and age *Fabulous*, we operate from a place of influence and inspire others to be so too, creating a potent ripple effect.

This makes it easier to become unavailable for any of the "isms." If we encounter them, we swiftly move along and go elsewhere. Where possible, we do not engage, acknowledge, or put up with them.

In the spirit of the *Fabulosity* movement, I hereby invite women in positions of authority to step into their Fabuli archetype, and to hire, coach, inspire and cheerlead their mature sisters. From there, we can change the world!

And we all know that the world desperately needs change. I believe the Dalai Lama had it right when he said:

> "The world will be saved by the Western woman."

I'm not sure why he specifies "Western" women, but I do know that if all women step into their power, everyone benefits.

So, looking young is not sustainable or possible, so Fresh is the new goal instead.

Looking Fresh is available to everyone, and it refers to your physical appearance as well as your spirit and attitude.

As with *Fabulosity*, Fresh is open to interpretation and is ever-evolving, but here are some ideas about what Fresh means to the Fabuli:

Intentional style

The clothes you wear have been carefully selected to make you feel sassy, and empowered. It's not about what's most flattering or what makes you look YTB. You know what patterns, fabrics, styles, and textures light you up, and your wardrobe is filled with "*Fabulous*" clothes, whatever that means to you.

Colors that you love

Wear colors because you love them, not because you've been told which ones are most complimentary, although the two are not mutually exclusive. The priority, however, is to please yourself and wear the colors that light you up. The joy that comes from this raises your vibration and inspires others, making a positive impact and radiating freshness and vitality.

Good grooming

A great haircut, cared-for hands and nails, and moisturized skin go a long way toward making you look Fresh, no matter what age or weight you are.

Natural or great make-up

Make-up is a miracle *Fabification* tool that can be used to create all manner of different energies.
The goal is to use makeup to help you bring You 2.0 to life, and to look *Fabulous*, not younger.

Great accessories that show your personality

Women are Christmas trees, not hangers. Accessories bring your personality out and give you a Fresh look. Find the treasures that turn an ordinary outfit into a spectacular one.

Glowing skin and energy

Fresh comes from looking after yourself, eating well, and moving your body. Pamper yourself with delicious-smelling soaps, fragrances, and creams, and enjoy these small luxuries every day. The energy that comes from amazing scents, looking after your body, and prioritizing daily pleasures is palpable.

Smiling

Who said, "You're never fully dressed without a smile?" A smile is infectious, making yourself and everyone around you feel better. Smile, baby, smile!

Positive about life

Someone who has an energy and "look" of freshness about them exudes positivity and effervescence. It's very attractive and inspiring, again raising the vibration of the world.

You don't need to *be* young or *look* young to have value or visibility. Aim for Fresh in everything—your outfits, outlook, routines, and vibration—so that your "lack of young" becomes completely irrelevant.

Remember: "Young" is not the same as "youth."

We can all benefit from having youth in our expression, outlook and energy, which, if you read between the lines, is inherent in *Fabulosity*.

FABULOUS

Fabulous is the second "F" in the FIFI Formula and the antidote to *thin*.

I'd like to illustrate this point with a simple visualization. Imagine you enter a crowded room, and as you walk in, everyone turns their heads to look at you, all gasping in awe and saying, "Wow, she's so... thin."

Isn't it more stupendous to enter a crowded room, and have everyone turn their heads to look at you, gasp, and say, "Wow, she's so *Fabulous?*"

Fabulous because you're wearing a great outfit.
Fabulous because you're obviously loving life.
Fabulous because you must be doing amazing things.
Fabulous because you make a difference in the world.
Fabulous because you're so confident in your own skin.
Fabulous for whatever reason, other than YTB!

When you show up *Fabulous*—in clothes that light you up, energy that is infectious, and a vibration that life is a big adventure—your body size is of absolutely no consequence. Whether you are fat or thin, it's completely irrelevant.

"*Fabulous*" in FIFI is the expression of your inner essences (personality, energy, and mindset) as well as the outer you (like your clothes, language, and behavior).

It's a representation of your empowered self-identity that has its roots in *Fabulosity*, You 2.0, and the archetype of the Fabuli.

If you swap the desire to be thin for the desire to be *Fabulous*, you'll probably exhibit some of the following:

You smile a lot.
You make eye contact.
You walk tall.
You take up space in the room.
You make people feel welcome.
You are liberal with genuine compliments.
You laugh at your faults and challenges.
You attract people.
You wear clothes that signify personality, confidence, and freedom.

When you "focus on *Fabulous*," you are taken so far away from the drive to be thin that thin no longer even features.

Remember that your body is the least interesting thing about you.

Repeat this over and over again until you know it in your bones. It's simply a canvas for your fascinating clothes, your zest for life, and your joy of experiencing everything this beautiful planet has to offer.

If all you see when you look in the mirror is what you deem to be flaws, those are all that others will see in you, and their own flaws will be exaggerated too.

The opposite is also true. If you see yourself as the incredible, awesome, significant, creature of magnificence that you are, so will others. And those who are blind to your *Fabulosity* don't matter! They are not your people!

Here are some of the practical elements of *Fabulous*:

Clothes

I don't care what anyone says; there is no doubt in my mind that clothes are a critical factor in how *Fabulous* a woman feels. I have yet to come across a woman for whom clothes do not play some role in her feelings of self-worth, whether she claims to have zero interest in clothes or the opposite.

The fashion industry is enormous, as we know, yet the focus we put on the clothes we wear is often deemed vanity or superficiality.

This is crazy to me because clothes are the most readily available tools we have to express our personality and individuality, even if we don't consider ourselves stylish or even interested in fashion.

Clothes are instrumental in presenting You 2.0. It's simply not possible to show up as a rock star if you wear track pants and flip-flops.

I'm an avid fan of Strictly Come Dancing, also known as Dancing With The Stars, and I remember one of the contestants saying that she was always very nervous for her dances until the moment when she emerged from the change room in her costume, wig, and make-up. As soon as she looked the part of a dancer, she became one on the inside, and she felt so much more ready to step onto the dance floor.

There's a lot of information out there about style, and many fashion gurus make it seem like style is something certain lucky people are born with.

Style is made out to be an art, and it's very complicated, so you need help from those in the know to get it "right." Heaven forbid if you get it wrong!

We don't have to look far to find someone telling us the rules—what to wear and what not to wear. On the whole, we are constantly fed the message that we must wear clothes that are age-appropriate, colors that suit us, and styles that are slimming or flattering. These rules and guidelines are all designed to make us more palatable to society's expectations.

> *I invite you to be discerning about what advice you allow in and make sure you implement only what supports You 2.0, regardless of what is considered stylish or fashionable.*

The only guideline you need is whether your clothes make you look, feel, and age *Fabulous*, whatever that means to you.

In terms of your dress size, it's none of your business what letter or number someone else uses in their manufacturing process. Your dress size should have no impact on how you feel about yourself, so remember that next time you shop for clothes.

At the end of the day, the only reason to lose weight is if it's affecting your health. In all other situations, dress up your body in *Fabulous* fashion, put a spring in your step, and enjoy your food.

Language

We touched on the power of language earlier in the book, but I'd like to explore it a little more here in the context of how *'Fabulous'* expresses itself practically.

It's a well-known fact that the language we use has powerful influences on our well being, happiness, and, dare we say it, our *Fabulosity*. And again, language is a habit.

If you want to have a more positive outlook on life, it's a good idea to use empowering words—words that make you feel strong, sassy, empowered, and capable.

For example, instead of saying your Summer holiday was "fine," words like "amazing" or "magical" are a lot more descriptive and interesting.

The energetic difference between the words "fine" and "amazing" is immense.

Anthony Robbins talks about "transformational vocabulary."

This means replacing negative words with more positive ones or using words that disrupt negative emotional patterns.

For example, instead of saying "it's impossible" about something you're trying to do, say "it's a little tricky." In this instance, reducing the intensity of your words creates possibility and opens up a pathway for a more empowering story where anything can happen.

At other times, you will want to increase the intensity, like in my example of Bruce earlier in the book, who never says "fine" when someone asks him how he is. He says, "I'm so fantastic, it's frightening." That statement is incredibly powerful.

It's important to remember that the words you use don't just affect you; they also affect the people around you.

If you want to be more charismatic and have more meaningful interactions with others, try to use positive, empowering language when you're talking with them.

They will feel more empowered and positive, too.

By the same token, be careful not to pick up negative words and behaviors from others, because they can affect you more than you realize. Make yourself unavailable for anything that is not empowering.

Body Language

Body language is language, and we want it to be *Fabulous*.

This means standing up straight with our shoulders back, making eye contact, and having an open posture. Standing this way not only makes us feel more emboldened and positive, but it also makes others perceive us as confident and approachable, which subconsciously empowers them to feel more confident and approachable.

I remember watching Amy Cudd's Ted Talk about the empowering nature of "power poses." This is where you stand with your feet apart and your arms raised above your head in a V shape.

She found that standing in the power pose for just two minutes can increase feelings of confidence and decrease levels of cortisol, the stress hormone.

Tony Robbins is big on this concept too, but he teaches it with a lot more testosterone in his expression! He says that your body and emotions are linked, so if you want to change your feelings, start by changing your physiology.

For instance, standing up straight makes you feel confident and awake, while slouching can make you feel down and tired. So whenever you're feeling sleepy or low, try standing up and taking deep breaths. Or dance. Or jump and shout. You can totally change your mood and mindset if you make a conscious effort to use your body in a positive way.

Body Neutralizing

Body Neutralizing is my replacement for "body positivity," because, although I think there is a place for body positivity, I have a slightly controversial view of it.

Body positivity is a movement that aims to reduce shame and promote self-love and acceptance of all body types, regardless of their size, shape, or appearance. It encourages people to embrace their bodies and celebrate their uniqueness.

I think this is a great message, and I support the idea that everyone deserves to feel confident and comfortable in their own skin without being judged or discriminated against based on their appearance.

However, I sometimes feel that this is yet another unrealistic expectation that society is putting on us.

I mean, I don't have a particularly positive view of how my body looks.

Do you?

I don't celebrate "its uniqueness" or "feel love for the lumps and bumps," especially when I see it in its naked form! Do you know of any women who do?

For me, I appreciate my body for what it allows me to do (swim, walk, do things, experience pleasure, wear Fabulous clothes), but I don't love how it looks.

What the FIFI Formula has taught me to do is be neutral about it. My body is simply a canvas and a vessel. As a canvas, it needs to be *Fabified* with gorgeous clothes, and as a vessel, it needs to be filled with a *Fabified* inner life, good food, and movement. I use it to express my identity. Nothing more. Nothing less.

It's not necessary to love my body in order to look and feel Fabulous.

I really appreciate the body positivity movement for standing up to the unrealistic beauty standards promoted by the media and society.

I agree that there needs to be more focus on the creation of a more accepting and supportive environment where everyone feels valued and respected, regardless of their physical appearance.

> *But let's not put pressure on ourselves to stand in front of the mirror in our underwear and pretend to embrace and love our flaws.*

Our bodies are the least interesting thing about us. They are the canvases that we've been given, and it's up to us to use clothes as our art materials to make them shine.

We don't need to love them. We don't need to look YTB to look *Fabulous*. And we don't need to wear clothes to please others.

Charisma

Charisma is a key trait exhibited by women who are self-confident, a.k.a. *Fabulous*.

Charisma is a compelling combination of inspiring qualities, including courage, positivity, and energy. These traits make a woman magnetic and attractive in her own eyes as well as in the eyes of others.

You might think that charisma is a trait that one is born with, but *Fabulosity* says this is not the truth.

> *Charisma can be learned by anyone who chooses to enter the Fabosphere in spectacular fashion.*

And like *Fabulosity*, charisma is not reserved for those who are extroverted or YTB.

So, how does charisma manifest?

Courage
Charismatic people exude courage and are comfortable in their own skin. They speak their minds and express their opinions.

Positive energy
Charismatic people tend to be upbeat and positive. They often have contagious enthusiasm that draws others to them.

Empathy
Charismatic individuals are able to connect with others on an emotional level. They are good listeners and are able to understand and empathize with alternative perspectives.

Authenticity
Charismatic people are genuine and comfortable with who they are, and where they are in life. They don't try to be something they're not, and they're not afraid to show vulnerability.

Presence
Charismatic people have a commanding presence. They are often very engaging and have a way of captivating an audience. This comes from a positive self identity and sheer love of life.

Good communication skills
Charismatic people are good communicators. They articulate their ideas clearly and are good at conveying their message in a compelling way.

Sense of humor
Charismatic people have a good sense of humor and are able to see the lighter side of life.

Overall, charismatic people exude *Fabulosity*, tend to be likable, and have a magnetic personality that draws people to them.

Charisma is available to all of us.

Focus On The Positive

It's been implied, but I'd like to emphasize here that if you focus on *Fabulous* instead of "thin," you are automatically creating the habit of positivity.

Positive people are happier people and are simply much better for the planet!

Focusing on the positive is not about pretending that everything is fine or sweeping issues under the carpet instead of dealing with them.

It's about consistently anticipating happiness, health, and success, instead of anticipating the worst.

Focusing on the positive is about looking at the bright side and finding the divine or stoic lesson in the challenge. It's about talking about what's good about life, rather than focusing on your problems. It's also about avoiding gossip, naysayers, and negativity.

Make yourself unavailable for the news, one of the scourges of modern society, which is designed to shock and instill fear.

Avoid drama, small-minded complainers, and unimportant trivia that makes you feel bad.

You won't be able to eliminate it all completely, but you'll feel a lot more hopeful and optimistic about life with less of it. And when you're positive about life, the size of your body is immaterial.

Grit

One of my favorite TED Talks is by the scientist, Angela Lee Duckworth, who did research on the predictors of success.

I was surprised to learn that it's not intelligence, wealthy parents, or any other advantage of birth or situation that will determine how well you get on in all aspects of life. Although these are helpful, Duckworth discovered that the one thing successful people have in common is grit.

Grit is officially defined as:

"courage and resolve; and strength of character,"

but Duckworth defines it as:

> *"passion and perseverance for very long-term goals."*

I love both of these definitions, and I think that people who could be deemed *Fabulous* would definitely demonstrate grit.

Everything Is Figureoutable

Just as "grit" is a *Fabulous* trait, so too is the attitude that "everything is figureoutable", a concept popularized by author and speaker Marie Forleo in her book of the same name.

The concept behind this phrase is that no matter what challenge or obstacle we face in life, there is always a solution or a way to work it out.

> *At its core, the philosophy that "everything is figureoutable" is centered on adopting a growth mindset and refusing to be defeated by setbacks or difficulties. .*

It's about approaching problems with a sense of curiosity, persistence, and a willingness to experiment and learn from failure.

This mindset can be incredibly empowering, as it allows us to take control of our circumstances and view obstacles as opportunities for growth and learning. It can also help us overcome limiting beliefs and self-doubt, which can often hold us back from pursuing our goals and dreams.

Of course, this doesn't mean that everything is easy or that we will always find a happy solution to every problem. But by embracing the idea that everything is figureoutable, we can develop the resilience and resourcefulness necessary to face challenges head-on, knowing things will work out, and that we will ultimately achieve our goals.

This is truly *Fabulous*.

Take Back Your Power

In this crazy thing we call life, there is always a mix of things that we can and cannot control. It's easy to confuse which is which, but if we remember that so often what we deem to be facts are actually just stories, it's easier to sift out the instances where we have the ability to take back power.

I'd like to illustrate this very important point with three short stories.

Mind Over Matter

During the time I was in a low mood, I expressed how I was feeling to a friend of mine who was a psychotherapist at the time. After listening to me for a few minutes, she told me that some people are just hard-wired to be depressed, and, wait for it, there is nothing to be done about it.

What? I couldn't believe my ears. That may be true in her experience and may well be the generally accepted view of depression among professionals, but I decided to create another story.

> *I would not allow depression to be my story for long.*

I was very grateful to her because her words inadvertently lit a fire in my belly to sort myself out. I took my power back.

The Story About Johanna

On my podcast, *"Fabulous To Meet You,"* I had the honor of interviewing Johanna, a remarkable young woman in her thirties whose story is truly incredible. About five years ago, a super-fit Johanna woke up one day with a migraine, paralysis on one side of her face, and difficulty swallowing.

Tests revealed that she had a brain tumor, and after many more tests and multiple medical consultations with different doctors, the prognosis was terrifyingly inconclusive and bleak, and the course of treatment was unclear.

> *Joanna was always a believer in positive thinking, and one of her friends challenged her to put her money where her mouth is and use positivity to help her heal herself.*

She took on this challenge in earnest and, despite feeling very fearful about the situation she was in, started to work on her mindset. She surrounded herself with joyful music, positive people, and uplifting energy, consistently visualizing herself as healed. Remarkably, her symptoms started to ease.

She began to exercise again, and as her body got stronger and stronger, she began to feel excited to hear good news from the doctor at her next consultation.

Despite her obvious progress, Johanna's follow-up doctor's visit was devastating. She learned that the tumor had not decreased in size and that there was still no clear course of treatment. On top of that, she was told to expect imminent facial disfigurement and vision loss.

Johanna was shocked to hear this because her body was showing clear signs of improvement. This bad news instantly put Johanna back into a state of fear and hopelessness, and almost immediately her unpleasant physical symptoms returned.

> *Despite feeling temporarily defeated, Johanna had solid proof that her "positivity bathing" and exercise were beating the symptoms, so she decided that she would no longer expect certainty and instead choose joy.*

She adopted the mindset that for as long as she could move her body, she would do so - every day - and she was going to live life to the full in absolute *Fabulous* fashion.

Fast forward five years, and Joanna is in the best shape of her life.

> *She gave up her job designing fliers for someone else, started her own kick-ass branding agency, and now spends her time pursuing all the adventurous activities that she loves.*

She hasn't seen a doctor again and has no interest in the existence, or non-existence of the tumor.

I'm not sharing this story to trivialize anyone's battle with disease and treatments, but there's a lot to love about Johanna's story.

What stands out for me is that she made the decision to take her power back!

The Trip To The Theater

My daughter was desperate to see a play at our local theater recently. Unfortunately, it was very quickly sold out, but having recently learned from a friend of mine to exercise more tenacity in the face of "no", we jumped in the car on the evening of the performance and, at the ticket office, two minutes before showtime, asked about cancellations or no-show tickets.

The lady was clearly put out by the request, mumbling that there weren't any, and there was a long waiting list.

With my friend's voice playing in my head, we were unperturbed, and we found a way to get to the theater foyer, where we walked up to the young man with a clipboard in his hand and asked the same question.

Without blinking, he ushered us in, happy to have people fill up the unclaimed seats, and we watched the show, thanking our lucky stars that (a) we took our power back by deciding to take a chance and (b) we asked the same question of two different people, getting different answers.

I'm sure we can all think of many instances in our lives where we gave away our power.

>Taking back your power is a *Fabulous* trait.
>Exercising tenacity is a *Fabulous* trait.
>Asking the same question of two different people is a *Fabulous* trait.
>Empowered women spend zero time worrying about their dress size.

Gosh, look at the time.

We're racing along, and soon the goal of looking young, thin, and beautiful (YTB) will be a thing of the past, thanks to the FIFI Formula.

We've done the two "F's", now let's move onto the "I's".

INTERESTING AND INTERESTED

As a recap, *Fresh* is the antidote to *young*, and *Fabulous* is the antidote to *thin*. Now onto the antidote to *Beautiful* which is the two "I"s in FIFI. They stand for *Interesting* and *Interested*.

Not many intelligent, successful women will admit to wanting to look beautiful, yet there is a multi-billion dollar beauty industry built on the purchases of women of all ages with exactly this aspiration. We want to look beautiful, or, put another way, make the most of ourselves.

It appears that human beings are designed to appreciate that which is aesthetically pleasing, and in today's society, the "beauty premium" is well-documented.

If given the choice, both women and men would probably choose to be attractive rather than not because, in general, attractive people are perceived as having more confidence, popularity, and success.

So, what do we do when our looks fade as we age or if we were born without the "beauty" gene? Should we yield to our more attractive sisters and give over to a life less *Fabulous*?

No!

We do not need beauty to be "attractive".

What we need instead is to embody *Interesting* and *Interested*. Let's start by exploring *Interesting* which, like all the elements of *Fabulosity*, is open to interpretation.

Officially, to be "interesting" means "to arouse curiosity," and "to hold or catch attention," but in the *Fabosphere* it's a combination of the external (such as how you dress) and internal (your personality).

Here are some examples of how *Interesting* (in the FIFI definition) might manifest:

> You wear inspiring, unique clothes that
> express your personality and verve.
>
> You have a clear point of view on things
> and are courageous enough to express it.
>
> You have compelling and stimulating
> topics of conversation, based on life
> experience, self-learning and interest.
>
> You are charismatic and fun to have around,
> lighting up the room with your presence.
>
> You are constantly in creation or exploration mode—
> initiating projects, events, learning, outings, and
> social engagements that stimulate conversation, discovery,
> fun, and personal growth for yourself and others.
>
> You are an excellent host, creating a safe,
> hospitable environment for your guests.
>
> You take your place in society, knowing
> your value, and the value of others.

To be *Interested* on the other hand, means you show curiosity or fascination for other people, or for topics outside of yourself. This is an incredibly attractive trait, and something that very charismatic people have in common.

In the FIFI definition, *Interested* might look something like this:

> You are curious about new people and experiences engaging with them and asking questions.
>
> You are also a great listener, seeking to understand the point of view of others.
>
> You actively look for opportunities to learn something new.
>
> You make people feel valued by inquiring about them.
>
> You are chatty and engaging in social situations, clearly enjoying yourself.
>
> You're fun to have around, adding value to whatever situation you find yourself in.

Someone who is *Interesting* and *Interested* becomes charismatic, compelling, and magnetic and doesn't need to be beautiful to attract or hold attention in a room, boardroom, social setting, or anywhere else.

FIFI Formula In Short

I don't know about you, but I'm done with trying to look Young, Thin and Beautiful (YTB) where I waste time, money, and energy on a pointless exercise that doesn't make me any happier; in fact, the opposite.

It was a happy day when I realized that to attract attention, be seen, be heard, and be relevant, I could simply be the most Fabulous version of myself.

The FIFI Formula is a practical guide to help me do that.

Aim for *Fresh*, not young.
It's pointless trying to look young with an aging face and body.

Aim for *Fabulous*, not thin.
Enjoy your food. Enjoy your life. Even with your larger body.

Aim for *Interesting* and *Interested* instead of beautiful.
When you explore all that this life has to offer and make people feel good, beauty is just not relevant.

FABULOSITY STARTS NOW

Conclusion

So there you have it: My invigorating perspective on how *Fabulosity* can help you look, feel and age *Fabulous*.

To recap, *Fabulosity* is neither an art nor a science. It's a habit and a life philosophy that inspires individuals to embrace their true selves and live life to the fullest.

This approach to life is meant to be a sort of pattern interrupter so that we can shake awake and strut! In other words, we can break free from the societal norms and expectations that can hold us back.

Fabulosity is a genial, flamboyant, and expansive take on self-actualization, confidence, and goal-setting.

It encourages individuals to focus on radical self-empowerment and find pleasure in everything they do.

It's not about achieving success or avoiding failure; it's about recognizing that every success and every failure is not good or bad; they are just *Fabulous*. They make us who we are.

One of the core beliefs of *Fabulosity* is that an expanded self-identity is critical to living a life in the *Fabosphere* (the energetic place where *Fabulous* people reside).

> *It is not about conforming to the expectations of others but rather discovering and shining as our true selves.*

Fabulosity encourages us to change our self-identity often, as it helps us grow and experience new things. Ironically, this helps us become more authentic.

When we embrace everything about ourselves and our lives, we reduce our fear and unleash our courage to express ourselves fully.

Self-expression in its most authentic and expansive form is invigorating, allowing us to live with lightness, curiosity, and a sense of adventure.

Fabulosity has three foundational tenets - Celebration, Reinvention and Fabification.

These help us to achieve many sensational, and ever-evolving outcomes, including freedom, pleasure, authenticity, spontaneity, confidence, and activation.

Fabulosity also has a big impact on the clothes we wear, inspiring us to dress for ourselves in outfits that light us up. It encourages individuals to stop trying to look young, thin, and beautiful to turn heads in any room. Instead, it inspires us to embrace our unique style and wear what makes us feel good which makes us look good.

The FIFI Formula is a key aspect of the *Fabulosity* philosophy. It kicks out the need for cosmetic surgery, fashion rules, and dieting, and instead, we focus on *Fresh, Interesting, Fabulous and Interested*.

With this formula, we no longer need to fear becoming invisible, irrelevant, or that our best years are behind us.

Instead, we can confidently and fabulously live life on our terms.

When we live with *Fabulosity* in midlife and beyond, we can call upon the Fabuli archetype to remind us that seniors have immense value to provide the world through their experience, energy, wisdom, and verve. They also have earned the right to enjoy their lives without being pressured to look or behave a certain way.

In summary, *Fabulosity* is a "*Fabulous*" approach to personal growth and happiness.

It aims to inspire you to discover
and craft expanded and compelling
versions of yourself.

It encourages you to play bigger, bolder, and
braver, and to break the rules.

Life is an Experiment.

Life is happening FOR you, not TO you.
Embrace it, live it with gusto, and
don't look back.

Thank you so much for being here with me. I hope that I've inspired you to adopt *Fabulous* as a way of seeing the world, and as a way of being in the world.

If you feel so inclined, let me know how you're getting on. Find me on LinkedIn and social media under my name or *Come Be Fabulous*.

Until next time, see you in the *Fabosphere*!

Yolanda Drewell

PART V

BONUS

The Rabbi's Gift

"The Rabbi's Gift" is a short story that has been attributed to various sources, but its origin is uncertain. It has been widely circulated on the internet and is often used as a teaching tool in schools and religious organizations.

●

There was a monastery that, despite once being a great order, had fallen on hard times and was clearly a dying order.

In the deep woods surrounding the monastery, there was a little hut that a rabbi from a nearby town occasionally stayed in. Through their many years of prayer and contemplation the old monks had become a bit psychic, so they could always sense when the rabbi was in residence.

"The rabbi is in the woods; the rabbi is in the woods again," they would whisper to each other.

As he agonized over the imminent death of his order, it occurred to the abbot to visit the rabbi for any advice that might save the monastery.

The rabbi welcomed the abbot to his hut, but when the abbot explained the purpose of his visit, the rabbi could only commiserate with him.

"I know how it is," he exclaimed. "The spirit has gone out of the people. It is the same in my town. Almost no one comes to the synagogue anymore."

So the old abbot and the old rabbi wept together. Then they read parts of the Torah and quietly spoke of deep things. The time came when the abbot had to leave. They embraced each other.

"It has been a wonderful thing that we should meet after all these years," the abbot said, "but I have still failed in my purpose for coming here. Is there nothing you can tell me, no piece of advice you can give me that would help me save my dying order?"

"No, I am sorry," the rabbi responded. "I have no advice to give. *The only thing I can tell you is that the Messiah is one of you.*"

When the abbot returned to the monastery, his fellow monks gathered around him to ask, "Well, what did the rabbi say?"

"He couldn't help," the abbot answered. "The only thing he did say, just as I was leaving—it was something cryptic—was that the Messiah is one of us. I don't know what he meant."

In the days, weeks, and months that followed, the old monks pondered this and wondered whether there was any possible significance to the rabbi's words.

> *The Messiah is one of us? Could he possibly have meant one of us monks here at the monastery? If that's the case, which one?*

Do you suppose he meant the abbot? Yes, if he meant anyone, he probably meant Father Abbot. He has been our leader for more than a generation.

On the other hand, he might have meant Brother Thomas. Certainly, Brother Thomas is a holy man. Everyone knows that Thomas is a man of light.

Certainly he could not have meant Brother Elred! Elred gets crotchety at times. But come to think of it, even though he is a thorn in people's sides, when you look back on it, Elred is virtually always right. Often very right. Maybe the rabbi did mean Brother Elred.

But surely not Brother Phillip. Phillip is so passive—a real nobody. But then, almost mysteriously, he has a gift for somehow always being there when you need him.

He just magically appears by your side. Maybe Phillip is the Messiah.

> *Of course, the rabbi didn't mean me. He couldn't possibly have meant me. I'm just an ordinary person. Yet supposing he did? Suppose I am the Messiah? O God, not me. I couldn't be that much for You, could I?*

As they contemplated in this manner, the old monks began to treat each other with extraordinary respect on the off chance that one among them might be the Messiah.

And on the off chance that each monk himself might be the Messiah, they began to treat themselves with extraordinary respect.

Because the forest in which it was situated was beautiful, it so happened that people still occasionally came to visit the monastery to picnic on its tiny lawn, to wander along some of its paths, and even now and then to go into the dilapidated chapel to meditate.

As they did so, without even being conscious of it, they sensed this aura of extraordinary respect that now began to surround the five old monks and seemed to radiate out from them and permeate the atmosphere of the place.

There was something strangely attractive, even compelling, about it. Hardly knowing why, they began to come back to the monastery more frequently to picnic, to play, and to pray.

They began to bring their friends to show them this special place. And their friends brought their friends. Then it happened that some of the younger men who came to visit the monastery started to talk more and more with the old monks. After a while, one asked if he could join them. Then another. And another.

So within a few years, the monastery had once again become a thriving order and, thanks to the rabbi's gift, a vibrant center of light and spirituality in the realm.

A final Note from the author

Isn't this a great illustration of the power of self-identity?

Self-identity is everything.

Once you decide, who you want to be, become that person as much as possible. If you have no idea, become the Queen of *Fabulosity* for starters and see a magical journey unfold.

Love and hogs
Yolanda

I'M SORRY.
PLEASE FORGIVE ME.
I FORGIVE YOU.
THANK YOU.
I LOVE YOU.

A variation on the spectacular Ho'oponopono
(Hawaiian prayer)

Help Others Find Their Fabulous

Thank you, Fabulista, for getting this far.

This book has been an exercise in putting my money where my mouth is. Never in a million years did I foresee that I would one day write a book, let alone one about how a word can change the world!

Without Fabulosity I would never have found the courage or persistence to get it out. This book is not perfect, but I let go of perfection a long time ago, and I've never looked back!

Just a reminder that a review on Amazon is a quick and easy way to help other women decide whether Fabulosity will help them create lives lived with lightness, curiosity, and a sense of adventure.

There are hundreds of searches on Amazon every month on the keywords "self-confidence for women," "self-esteem for women," "successful aging" and similar. Women are looking for inspiration to break free from their own limitations and those imposed by society. This book may well be a life-changer for them.

It's a Fabulous trait to ask for what you want, so I would be tickled orange if you would leave a review (anonymous or not) on Amazon, with five stars, and if possible, with or without a screenshot or video (easy to do). Five stars and a review will help my book succeed because Amazon rates reviews and 5 stars above all else.

Also, don't forget to stay connected with the Fabosphere. You can do that on our website yolandadrewell.com/lfaf

Until next time, rock on with your Fabulous self!
Yolanda

Other Books
By Fabulous Publishing Co

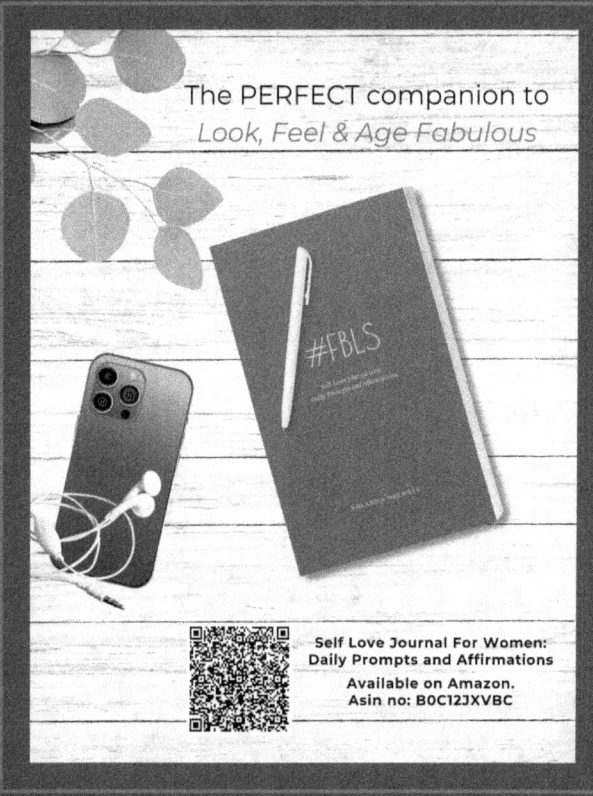

**Self Love Journal For Women:
Daily Prompts and Affirmations**

Available on Amazon.
Asin no: B0C12JXVBC

Resources

Ackerman, C. E., MA. (2023). What Is Neuroplasticity? A Psychologist Explains [+14 Tools]. PositivePsychology.com. https://positivepsychology.com/neuroplasticity/

Advanced Style. (2023, March 23). Advanced Style. https://www.advanced.style/

Akhtar, D. B. a. A. (2019, October 8). 11 scientific reasons why attractive people are more successful in life. Ladders | Business News & Career Advice. https://www.theladders.com/career-advice/11-scientific-reasons-why-attractive-people-are-more-successful-in-life

Amy Porterfield | Online Marketing Expert. (2023, February 18). Amy Porterfield | Online Marketing Expert. https://www.amyporterfield.com/

Angela Duckworth. (n.d.). Angela Duckworth. https://angeladuckworth.com/grit-book/

Atlantic Records. (2017, December 8). Come Alive [Video]. YouTube. https://www.youtube.com/watch?v=BURBlSYPmBU

AZLyrics - request for access. (n.d.). https://www.azlyrics.com/lyrics/greatestshowmancast/comealive.html

Carney, D. R., Cuddy, A. J. C., & Yap, A. J. (2010). Power Posing. Psychological Science, 21(10), 1363–1368. https://doi.org/10.1177/0956797610383437

Ecommerce Courses Online | Alison J. Prince. (2022, August 8). Alison J Prince. https://www.alisonjprince.com/

Everything is Figureoutable Gets a Whole New Look. (n.d.). https://www.marieforleo.com/blog/everything-is-figureoutable-paperback

Fortin, J. (2022, June 10). EPISODE 71: "You Can Uplevel The BE-DO-HAVE Model Using Identity Transformation" - JimFortin.com. JimFortin.com. https://www.jimfortin.com/episode-71-you-can-uplevel-the-be-do-have-model-using-identity-transformation/

Grinde, B., & Husselman, T. (2022). An Attempt to Explain Visual Aesthetic Appreciation. Integrative Psychological and Behavioral Science. https://doi.org/10.1007/s12124-022-09701-8

Kathryn Porritt. (n.d.). https://www.kathrynporritt.com/

Lowen, L. (2019). The Dalai Lama - "The World Will Be Saved By the Western Woman" ThoughtCo. https://www.thoughtco.com/dalai-lama-world-saved-western-woman-3971297

Making your first $100k Without Social Media. (n.d.). https://podcasts.apple.com/gb/podcast/making-your-first-$100k-without-social-media/id1199101868?i=1000586261097

Not only do micro influencers drive more conversions, but with their highly targeted audience they can produce a 20% higher conversion rate than bigger influencers at a significantly lower price. Often leading to better ROI overall. (n.d.). https://prohibitionpr.co.uk/category/digital-marketing/influencer-marketing/

Psycho-Cybernetics - See Yourself at Your Best. (n.d.). https://www.psycho-cybernetics.com/

Robbins, T. (2022, April 29). 4 steps to change your words, change your life | Tony Robbins. tonyrobbins.com. https://www.tonyrobbins.com/mind-meaning/change-your-words-change-your-life/

Susanna. (2020, April 15). The 12 Jungian Archetypes. Exploring Your Mind. https://exploringyourmind.com/twelve-jungian-archetypes/

Technicolor Priestess (2022). (n.d.). Technicolor Priestess (2022). https://www.technicolorpriestess.com/

TED. (2021, April 30). The strongest predictor for success | Angela Lee Duckworth [Video]. YouTube. https://www.youtube.com/watch?v=GfF2eovyGM4

Tony Robbins - The Official Website of Tony Robbins. (2019, March 21). tonyrobbins.com. https://www.tonyrobbins.com/

Tony, T. (2023, January 19). 6 human needs: why are they so important? tonyrobbins.com. https://www.tonyrobbins.com/mind-meaning/do-you-need-to-feel-significant/

Villines, Z. (2022a, August 30). What is shadow work? What to know. https://www.medicalnewstoday.com/articles/what-is-shadow-work

Villines, Z. (2022b, August 30). What is shadow work? What to know. https://www.medicalnewstoday.com/articles/what-is-shadow-work

Voip101. (2009, February 26). Time Theme [Video]. YouTube. https://www.youtube.com/watch?v=eWXAiLy786A

www.ingramcontent.com/pod-product-compliance
Lightning Source LLC
Chambersburg PA
CBHW071348080526
44587CB00017B/3012